# THE
# GREAT
# WHEELCHAIR
# ESCAPE

# THE
# GREAT
# WHEELCHAIR
# ESCAPE

## ROBERT MILLER'S TRUE STORY

DON CROWELL JR.

Cover Design by Steven Novak
Book design by Maureen Cutajar

*For Mom*
*Bill and Paul*

## *Special Thanks to*

My wife Mony, and all my beautiful children and grandchildren

Paul, Mom, Fred, Bill, and Señor Q for their contributions

Mary Coulter and the families' of 1732 Inc…
who really did make a difference

The good people of Mazatlan,
who cared enough to help.

For the prayers that were answered
and those who never lost faith

# Contents

# 1

## *Countdown*

The alert signs flashed on. *Abrocha Cinturón.* Time to buckle up. I reached for my seat belt as the pilot announced our approach to the airport outside Mazatlán. His words brought a boisterous cheer from the passengers, a mixed group of Mexican residents and American tourists. The flight was nearly thirty minutes late, but no one seemed to care. Cheers turned to choruses of olé as glasses of airline liquor and hidden reserves of tequila were hoisted in final toasts.

Below, I could see the green vegetation that surrounded the landing area; fields of corn with chile and lush orchards heavy with mango. Beyond, coming up fast, were the craggy slopes of Rock Island (*La Isla de la Piedra*) and the hotels of the Mexican Riviera. They stood bright in the hot July sun. It would be good to get back to this beautiful resort town, to its warm friendly people, and the carnival atmosphere I'd left only months earlier.

The plane landed, and after a lengthy wait I had my suitcases in hand. No one ever seemed to be in a hurry at the Mazatlán airport.

Heading toward the taxi stand, I spotted the middle-aged American couple who'd sat next to me during the flight. It was their first visit deep into Mexico and they were apprehensive about the water, the heat, the humidity, and the stereotype characters they'd seen over the years in Hollywood movies. Recent newspaper reports about "vanishing Americans" didn't add to their comfort. I had tried to reassure them.

"You'll look back on this trip with beautiful memories," I told them. "Now's the time to see Mazatlán, before it becomes another Acapulco." I waved to the couple and called,

"Have a great time."

"You too," the woman answered. "Don't get in any trouble."

I laughed. Her words sounded so improbable.

"Taxi *Señor*?" A brown-skinned Mexican in his early twenties with a wide grin on his face was at the wheel of a Volkswagen with a sawed-off top. He was wearing a t-shirt with "El Marinero" written across the front.

"Felix…you're moving up in the world," I replied, looking at the VW.

"Ay Roberto, I wish it was my car, but Rogelio let me borrow it, to pick you up."

I unzipped my suitcase and pulled out a loud Hawaiian shirt as Felix's eyes widened.

"I didn't forget."

Felix hopped out of the VW to grab the shirt and held it in front of him.

"What do you think?" he said smiling.

"Definitely you," I laughed. "People are starting to stare. Let's get a move on."

I threw my suitcase in the back and hopped in next to him.

"How's everything at the restaurant?"

"Packed full of tourists and beautiful *señoritas*. I met a special one who you're going to meet."

"What about Estela?"

"You got a winner there, Roberto. What did you do to her?"

"It's chemistry mano, chemistry. You didn't tell her I was coming?

"No way. She's going to the Mauna Loa tomorrow night with Blanca and has no idea you're in town."

Thirty minutes later we were on the *Malecón*, a beachside avenue, heading south toward hotel row. As I looked around, I recognized *Olas Altas*; the street seemed relatively lifeless now without the dancing revelers and wandering musicians that had filled the town during Carnival.

For me, Mazatlán was a magical place. Called the "Pearl of the Pacific", it's welcoming ocean and happy people were irresistible. During *Carnaval* and *Semana Santa* (Easter Week), it attracted visitors from all over Mexico, Canada, and the United States. During these periods a festive spirit danced through the town, while laughter and music filled the air.

As we drove, my thoughts went back to Estela and walking with her on the beach under thousands of stars. We had been corresponding by mail, and I was looking forward to seeing her again. I had a week in town before heading to the Instituto Allende for courses in Spanish and Archaeology. This would be the time to relax and enjoy myself before my studies began in earnest.

Felix pulled up in front of the lobby at the Hotel Playa Mazatlan–my favorite place to stay in town. It offered one of the best beaches, a friendly staff, and good food. I loved listening to the sound of waves breaking on the ocean as I was lulled to sleep at night.

"See you tomorrow at the restaurant," I said as he handed me my bag.

"*Simón* Roberto, I'll set everything up with the girls."

Felix knew my routine. I would always begin with my customary dip in the ocean; swimming and bodysurfing to unwind. Refreshing and rejuvenating. Afterwards, I was ready for anything the evening might bring. Time to make that phone call to Ron and Nancy.

A few weeks earlier in San Diego, my friend Dave had introduced me to Ron and Nancy at the bar of the Rueben E Lee. During our conversation I learned that Ron owned a Mercedes dealership in San Diego and was investing in tourism on the Mexican Riviera. Nancy had completed the same Archaeology course at the Instituto Allende that I had enrolled in. She offered to give me some recommendations and contact numbers in San Miguel de Allende. We had made tentative plans to get together in Mazatlán, since they would be staying at the nearby Hotel Playa del Rey.

I was connected to their room at the hotel and Ron answered the phone. He told me that Nancy had returned home, but he had remained in town another day to "close a deal." I accepted his invitation for dinner that evening at *Señor* Frog's, a Mexican-American-type restaurant that catered mainly to young, hip locals and the tourist trade. It wasn't my favorite place to eat, but the atmosphere was lively and everybody seemed to have a good time. Instead of a taxi, I would take a souped-up golf cart with music blaring, called a *Pulmonia*. I negotiated a price and climbed in; riding with my hair in the wind, while rock and roll music blasted out the speaker.

I spotted Ron immediately at the bar, not from his height (I'm six feet and he was a good two inches shorter), but from his flashy clothes and jewelry that stood out, just as when I had met him with Dave. He had the look of money and carried himself with assurance.

From the start, Ron made it clear he was running the show. When I tried to buy a round of drinks, he flashed a roll of bills and said, "I invited you, remember?" The talk centered exclusively around topics that interested him: his income, his real estate business, investments, and his car dealership in San Diego. I saw snapshots of his Mercedes, sexy Nancy in a swimsuit, and his racehorse. His commitment to Nancy was definitely not total, as he was ready to move in on a young lady nearby when we were informed that our table was ready.

We were finishing our meal when Ron saw a familiar face. "Lopez," he cried, reaching out to grab the man's arm. "Come join us."

Lopez sat down and Ron ordered Presidente (Brandy) on the rocks for the three of us.

"Meet Roberto, my good friend from the States," he said to the man. Turning to me, Ron added, "Lopez rents cars. If you need one, he'll take care of you. Right, amigo?"

Lopez reached into his wallet, pulled out a business card and handed it to me.

The young waiter returned with our drinks. No sooner had he left than Ron spotted some friends of his at another table outside on the patio. "I'm going out," he announced. "There's more action there."

By the time Lopez and I caught up with Ron, he was buying drinks for two other friends. One was Gustavo, a boyish-looking attorney. The other was Alfonso. I never learned what Alfonso did, but I heard mention of his father, who I deduced from the conversation, was the Mayor.

Ron, was coming on stronger than ever, trying to impress with his wealth and sexual prowess. His language grew embarrassingly crude and obnoxious. When he started making indecent gestures to any lady who casually glanced his way, Gustavo suggested I help take him outside. A taxi was waiting near the entrance.

"Capri, por favor," Gustavo instructed the driver.

"You'll like it there," Alfonso told Ron. He looked at Gustavo and smiled. As the car pulled away from the restaurant, I realized that Lopez had been left behind, perhaps by choice.

The Capri was on the outskirts of town in "*la zona roja*", the red zone. Mazatlán's most popular bordello, it offered the best show around. It attracted many customers from the surrounding ranches and farms. Some of the boisterous clientele wore tight Levis and sweat-soaked shirts, unbuttoned to the waist, with leather stomping boots. But there were others, far more sophisticated, who could not resist the steamy atmosphere and intrigue.

These were the locals of position, government workers, and occasionally a few tourists. Dressed in neatly pressed shirts and slacks, they stood out like royalty and were treated as such.

Except for a bank of fluorescent black lights behind the bandstand, the room was virtually dark when we arrived. That didn't stop Ron. He groped his way to a choice table in front of the entertainment area, leaving us three to follow.

Like flies attracted to a feast, scantily clad prostitutes swarmed to greet us, eyes narrowing at the prospect of easy money. Only one survived. She looked the oldest—early thirties—but was probably much younger. Certainly, she was the biggest—and tough as hide. The other girls, giving away at least ten years and fifty pounds, were no match and scattered at the sight of her. She stood next to Ron, toyfully playing with the gold chains and medallions that dangled about his neck.

Then she leaned over, just enough to let her enormous breasts hang loose. "We go to my place," she said in broken English. "I have bed in back. I show you everytheeng."

Ron moistened his lips and leaned forward.

The woman straightened quickly. "Two dollars to kees'm," she said flatly. "One dollar each."

"No mama, you pay me to kiss those big melons. I will drive you crazy," he laughed.

Now she was at my side. The pungent odor of cologne mixed with her perspiration did not captivate me. I felt her hand settle on the inside of my thigh and begin to move upward. I grabbed her wrist and looked hard into her eyes. Stunned by the recognition, she smiled sullenly and retreated. I stood and started to move away.

"Where are you going?" Gustavo asked.

"The *baño*," I replied.

"Follow me."

We crossed the darkened room, through the maze of tables and bodies, until we reached a door on the far side. Scratched into the dingy, paint-peeled surface was the word *Hombres*. Gustavo waited outside while I entered. The floor of the tiny, unventilated room was wet and littered with rotting paper. I held my breath and pissed.

I rejoined Gustavo quickly. "Whew! The fumes in there are potent."

"The Capri is a paradise compared to many clubs down the road in *Campo Siete*. And there's always *mordida* if the officials complain."

"*Mordida*?"

"We have a saying," Gustavo answered. "If an official-dies rich, he's a crook. If he dies poor, he's stupid. *Mordida* is a way of life in my country, a part of the system."

"We have a saying too—"money talks.""

Gustavo led me toward the back exit, past the bandstand now filling with musicians, and outside. We entered a courtyard planted with rose bushes. They were in bloom and the sweet aroma of fresh flowers erased the smells of the nightclub.

"Many of the girls live here," Gustavo said, pointing to the pink, two-story structure that walled the garden on three sides. "The rooms are small and fairly clean. These girls don't have such a bad life compared to the old days. I've seen records that would make you sick; how madams sent their helpers into the interior to kidnap young muchachas, girls in their early teens. They were sold to houses like this. Those who didn't cooperate were beaten until they changed their minds."

"In the old days?" I questioned, "Last trip here I heard something that made me sick. A couple of *vaqueros* were talking about picking up a fourteen-year old off the street and bringing her to the rancho for their *Patrón*."

"Unfortunately, there are still some that believe in the old ways. Here and in most reputable places the girls have a choice. They come voluntarily to make money to feed their children and help their families. Many customers are lonely men who need companionship and are willing to pay for it. If they hit it off, they become regulars, friends, and sometimes husbands."

An attractive young girl, no older than seventeen, walked by with her arm around a grizzly farmhand. She led him up a flight of stairs and into one of the rooms.

When Gustavo and I returned to our table, the band was playing and a ragged chorus line of four girls, covered only with shiny pasties and G-strings, moved mechanically about the floor, bumping and grinding to a heavily accentuated beat. Their faces were without expression, oblivious to the roaring cheers and applause of the crowd. Alfonso sat drinking quietly. Ron reacted by jumping up from time to time and shouting obscenities toward the stage. Only a blackout softened the roar. But the ensuing announcement by an unseen male voice created an even greater one.

"Presente . . . *la exotica* Pina Mia."

A rosy spotlight flickered on, revealing the star of the evening, a leggy Las Vegas-type showgirl with smooth, tawny skin, a small waist and ample breasts and long, silky black hair that she tossed like a whip. Dressed in the briefest of costumes and spike heels, Pina Mia had only to stand centerstage to raise the fever of the campesinos.

"*Ay yi yi, mamacita,*" they chanted as the band started a slow, romantic ballad in ranchero style.

Pina Mia, with the grace of a ballerina, appeared to float about the floor. The other girls may have thought it necessary to sock across their sensuality, but Pina played it more subtly. No vibrations, no gestures, no tantalizing movements. That lasted for the first few minutes of her act. Then, as the musicians picked up tempo, the mood changed abruptly. Pina began to work the tables, sliding up to the hungriest looking customers; sitting on their laps and shaking her breasts in their faces as they almost copped a feel. If anyone made a direct pass or got physical, she'd straighten and shout, "*Pinche Cabrón.*"

She had hit five tables and was approaching ours when Ron intercepted her, waving a twenty-dollar bill in her face. Alfonso pulled his arm down, but he raised it again.

"Easy money," Ron said, "forget it."

Pina slowly slipped the bill from Ron's hand, showed it to the howling mob and placed it between her lips. Taking Ron by the ear, she led him to center stage where she unfastened his belt and pulled it loose. Ron stood motionless, letting the lady work. It was difficult to tell if he was drunk, transfixed, or afraid of what might come next.

She placed his hands behind his back, tied them together with his belt, then forced him to his knees. The brassy music was increasing in volume when Pina stood directly before Ron, gyrating to the music. She spread her legs. With one hand behind his head and the other on the small floral triangle that covered her crotch, she was about to press his face against her body. Then the lights went out. When they came on again, Ron was alone on the floor. Still kneeling, he looked somewhat surprised. Immediately, he became the object of hoots, howls, and whistles.

We decided to call it a night. As we were walking out, I felt a pair of eyes through the smoke-filled air staring intently at us. I could barely make out the hazy outline of two figures moving in our direction and heard a slight clicking sound. As we reached the car I looked back and saw nothing. Must have been my imagination. Back in my room, all thoughts left me as I passed out instantly on the bed.

I was awakened by frantic pounding on my door. Who would call at this hour? I asked myself, thinking I'd just closed my eyes. I hadn't; it was eleven o'clock. I staggered to the door, and found Ron waiting.

"I need your help," he said, hurriedly.

I let him in and flopped back on the bed as he talked. His rented car, an orange Volkswagen Safari, was at *Señor* Frog's. He'd returned to get the car, but it wouldn't start. He had a taxi waiting in front and had to leave immediately for the airport to catch his flight home.

I got up and pulled open the drapes. The sun was bright and the temperature already in the mid-80s. People were on the beach, sunning and swimming. I was eager to join them.

"Do me a favor," Ron said. "Put some gas in the car and return it to Lopez. I've tried calling, but he's not in."

He held out the keys and a portfolio which he said contained the rental papers and phone number. "If you can't get him today," he said, reaching into his pocket for gas money, "use the car and call tomorrow, but get it in before I get charged for another day."

The thought of having a car for the day was appealing. I told him I'd handle it and set the keys, money, and portfolio on the dresser. Ron was already out the door.

After breakfast, I waved down a *Pulmonia*, rounded up a full gas can, and rode to the abandoned Safari. With a little fuel and some priming, it started right away. I drove around town to get my bearings, then spent the afternoon enjoying the warm waters of the Pacific. Nobody answered the phone at the Lopez number Ron had given me.

Felix worked at a popular seafood restaurant called El Marinero. I had already arranged to dine there before heading out to meet our dates. They would be waiting for us at the Mauna Loa, a popular night club with live dance music. I was looking forward to meeting Felix's new lady friend, but most of all to see Estela again. We had made a special connection on my last trip to Mazatlán and had been writing each other for months.

After a delicious dinner of shrimp *culichi* and a couple of Pacificos to wash them down, I was ready to give Felix a ride to the nightclub in the Safari.

"Just a minute," Felix said, as he went to the back of the restaurant and returned wearing the loud Hawaiian shirt, I had brought him.

"Whoa, you might get in trouble with that on. The ladies will be all over you."

"*Bueno*, as long as Blanca is one that catches me," he laughed, giving me a high five.

At the entrance, I stopped to read the show cards. Two bands, Sammy's People and Los Aztucas, were appearing nightly. As we started down a flight of stairs, we passed Carlos, the doorman and a fixture at the Mauna Loa for years. He was talking with a small group of men with his back to me. I didn't think he'd seen me.

"*Un momento*," a stern voice called. "You can't go down there."

Carlos came running after me.

"What do you mean?" I was shocked.

He started laughing.

"Roberto," he said, half whining as if I'd hurt his feelings, "you forget I like to play joke?"

"Sorry, Carlos," I smiled. "It's been awhile." He patted my shoulder and returned to his post.

Subconsciously, I expected to find the club as I remembered it during *Semana Santa*; long lines at the bar, every table filled, and the dance floor packed. But it wasn't that way tonight. The main room was only half full, less than a hundred people, a mixture of young American tourists and well-dressed locals. We moved around the dance floor and I spotted Estela, at a table with another young lady who I assumed was Felix's new heartthrob. Estela eyes opened wide in surprise as we approached the table. Blanca was an attractive young lady with light skin and green eyes. As Felix introduced me, I held out my hand and she took it.

"It's really good to meet you," I said, "Felix is happier than I can remember, and I think it has something to do with you."

"He told me some good things about you too."

As Estela stood up, I took in her welcoming smile and long black hair. Our eyes communicated as the romantic ballad "*Eres Tu*" started playing. I took her hand and we almost floated to the dance floor. Her closeness was magical to me and she obviously felt the same.

"I wondered why Blanca was so insistent that I come tonight."

She faked a punch to my stomach. "You almost gave me a heart attack."

"Your heart seems fine now."

"Maybe just beating a little faster than normal…but good."

I squeezed a little tighter as we moved to the music.

Back at the table the four of us ordered a couple of rounds and shared stories. Blanca was enrolled at a University, majoring in tourism and learning English. Estela was a teacher and had a group of students under her wing for summer studies. Felix was working at the restaurant while trying to get his pilot's license. We laughed together and danced with our partners, without a care in the world.

Estela finally came back to earth and reminded me she couldn't stay out late. She was helping her mother with preparations for her younger sisters *Quinceañera*, a celebration for her 15th birthday and coming of age. It was a huge *fiesta* in Mexico.

"You're invited," she told me with a smile.

"Wouldn't miss it for the world. I can give you a ride home anytime you're ready."

Felix and Blanca were already heading back to the dance floor. As Estela and I were leaving, Carlos the doorman nodded and winked at me.

# 2

## Night of Terror

s we approached the car, I opened the passenger door and our lips met in a long kiss. I entered through my side and was just about to start the car, when I heard a tapping at my window. A beam of light was shining in my eyes; then a louder pounding. I heard a voice speaking in Spanish.

"*Policia Federal*—Open the door!" A chrome plated forty-five revolver was pointing at my head.

"Get out!" the voice ordered.

Another light was directed at Estela and a command to open her door, "*Abre la puerta, Policia Federal!*"

A sudden shiver of fear raced through my body. I froze, then thought of Estela.

"This must be some mistake," I said, trying to sound calmer than I felt. "Let's get out and set them straight."

I started to open my door, but they weren't waiting. Before we could move, the doors were opened, our arms were grabbed, and we were pulled out of the car. There were three of them. The one on my side had a thick scar on his left cheek and a younger mustached partner stood beside him. Estela was brought over by the third—short and stocky.

"What's going on? What do you want?" I asked.

He ignored my questions and moved around me. I was pushed against the car by the younger one who patted me down quickly.

"I'm an American. You're making a mistake."

"Gordo, *la chavala*." The scar-faced leader told the stocky one to search the girl.

"*Si Jefe*," he replied as he purposely patted Estela down, and was obviously doing more than searching.

"Keep your hands off her." I moved to stop him.

Jefe and his young partner slammed me against the car.

Jefe put his gun to my head as he told his partner to check inside my pockets. My wallet and room key were now in his hand.

"*El coche!*" He ordered the younger one to look in the car. The floor mats were pulled out and every inch of the car was searched. Even the fabric that lined the doors and the ceiling were slit. The young one found nothing and shrugged his shoulders.

Jefe stared at me with an evil smile.

"You're not getting away this time, Ron. We know all about what you've been doing."

Estela pulled away from her captor. "This is Roberto, not Ron. You have the wrong man!"

Jefe just looked at her and smiled. He spit on the ground.

"Look, I have a right to know what's going on," I said.

"You have no rights in Mexico."

"Read my ID and you will see I am Robert, not the man you're looking for," I told him. "Ron gave me the keys to his car before he left for the airport."

As he looked at my driver's license, I felt more confident.

"Fake ID's are easy to come by. Where's the plane?"

"What plane? The one I came in? It dropped me and other tourists at the airport two days ago. How in the hell am I supposed to know where it is?"

"Don't be smart with me. You will tell me everything."

"Cuff him and put him in the car," he ordered the younger assistant.

"No!" shouted Estela pleading "Let him go. He has done nothing wrong"

"Now we will see what your friends inside have to say."

As he left, I heard a clicking sound caused by the metal on the bottom of the left shoe, as he walked with a slight limp.

I was handcuffed and put into the back seat of a Volkswagen. The young Fed went to join Jefe and Gordo at the nightclub. As I looked out the window, I could see them talking to the doorman, Carlos, and nodding in my direction. Gordo was holding Estela's arm.

I had to get out. I stretched my legs and used my feet, trying to pull and pry to open the front door. It wouldn't budge. I kicked at the door, then the window... nothing.

I looked out and could see Blanca and Felix in front with the Feds. Soon the girls were walking away and the three Feds were surrounding Felix and pointing to me. They began roughing him up and he went down. As he rose, I could see his bloody lip. He quickly shoved Gordo into Jefe and took off running. Jefe pulled out his forty-five and fired at the fleeing Felix, and missed. I watched the younger Fed take off after him on foot. Jefe and Gordo hurried to the car I was in, started it up, and headed in their direction. Jefe had the passenger window open and the gun ready to fire.

"You guys are nuts," I said. "They're my friends. They haven't done anything."

"*Callete cabrón*," Jefe angrily told me to shut up.

"*Apurate*," he told the driver hurry up, as we sped off in pursuit.

We soon caught up with the younger Fed who had taken off on foot behind Felix. He pointed to one of the unlit side streets and entered the car as we headed in that direction. After driving up and down the street, shining their flashlights towards all dark areas with no luck, they finally gave up. Jefe was holding my room key in his hand with the hotel name and my room number on it.

"Hotel Playa," he ordered the driver.

As we pulled up in front of the hotel, Jefe and Gordo got out.

"Let me go with you," I pleaded, "I haven't done anything."

"We will see," Jefe sneered.

Thirty minutes later they were back. The portfolio Ron had left me was in Jefe's hand. I knew it didn't take that long to go to my room and back, so they must have searched it well.

"Now that you searched my room, you know there is no reason to hold me."

With a sadistic smile Jefe said, "You will tell me everything…. Ron Warren," and he held up the rental papers in Ron's name. He also held up what appeared to be a joint of marijuana.

"I'm not Ron!" I told him. "and I don't even smoke." I realized all of this was happening because I was driving Ron's rented Safari.

"Listen, all you have to do is ask Lopez. He rented the car to Ron. The man you're looking for went to the airport and flew home."

"You think I'm stupid enough to believe that. Before the night is over, you will tell us everything."

"*La Escondida*," he ordered the driver to go to the hidden spot.

We drove out of town to a deserted field and pulled into a grassy area hidden from sight. Next thing I knew, the doors were opening and I was being pulled from the car. I landed on the grass, belly down. Then I was yanked to my feet by Jefe's assistants while he pointed his forty-five at me.

"Where do you get the marijuana?" he asked, "Who sells it?"

"I don't know."

He nodded to Gordo, who pulled out a switchblade and held it to my throat.

"You still don't know, Gringo?"

"I'm on my way to study at the Instituto Allende. The papers are in my room. Believe me, I'm telling the truth," I said.

"Don't lie to me. We know all about you and your associates. You must tell me what I need to know to be free."

Somebody snapped my head back and as I looked at the heavens above, I could see thousands of stars…shimmering pinpoints against the blackest night sky I could remember. I had heard of Americans disappearing in Mexico and pictured myself dying in this isolated field, never to be heard of again.

A flurry of blows landed on my chest, arms, and kidneys. I was brought down by a rock-hard punch in the pit of my stomach.

"Give me the names of your *socios--Digame!*" said Jefe.

I could hardly breathe, much less talk, even if I had known the answers to his questions.

"*La Chicharra,*" ordered Jefe, as Gordo hurried to the car and opened the trunk. He returned with an electric cattle prod.

The younger Fed ripped my shirt open and the two of them held me up from the sides. I felt a shock first between my ribcage, then on my nipple, more painful than anything I could remember. I screamed loudly into the dark desolate night.

"Give me the names!" Jefe insisted.

I held up my hand to have him stop and buy some time.

"OK, I'll give you some names," I said, still trying to recover from the plummeting and electric shocks.

"I met an attorney named Gustavo, and Lopez from the rental car company. There was another man, but I don't know his name. They are friends of Ron's. You're wasting your time with me."

"Ay, the *pajarito* is beginning to sing," said Jefe. "Let's hear the whole song."

"Take me to the American consulate. I have rights."

"You have no rights. You *Americanos* come to Mexico with your dollars and you tempt the poor people to grow your drugs. Now your government is paying us to stop you…. and we will."

"*Pantalones!*" ordered Jefe.

They pulled off my pants and I stood completely naked under the stars. Their eyes surveyed me, as Jefe with gleam in his eyes, teasingly waved the stick in my direction.

"*Chicharra's* going to teach you a lesson and you be like a talky old woman."

"*Juevos!*" as he aimed the metal rod at my testicles.

# 3

## Mexican Soldiers

**W**as I dreaming? My mind was in a haze and thoughts were blurry. As I slowly opened my eyes, I could feel an aching all over my body; arms, chest and stomach; my skin was burning….and oh my god, the family jewels, swollen up like softballs.

I was lying in the back of a car and could barely make out a head under the sombrero in the front seat. As I moved and attempted to sit up, the head turned to look at me. I could see his face and I recognized the young mustached *Federale*. He was obviously unconcerned since I was handcuffed and had great difficulty in sitting up. Struggling, I finally made it up to sitting position and looked out the window. Small private planes lined the runway. I could see a large Mexicana plane in the distance. We were at the Mazatlán airport where I had arrived just a couple of days earlier. Must be checking out my story. Now they would know I was telling the truth about Ron. Even with the pain, my spirits were lifted.

Soon Jefe and Gordo arrived outside of the car talking in Spanish. I strained my ears and thought I could make out Ron's name. A Ford Galaxy with California plates pulled up beside them. The driver, who appeared to be American, was talking to Jefe as if they were old friends. After a few minutes the Galaxy left and the two Feds walked to the car. Gordo took the driver's seat and the younger one moved next to me, as Jefe took his seat, riding shotgun.

"Now you know I was telling the truth and Ron has left. If you let me go, I'll be quiet and no one will know about your mistake."

The car started up.

"Are you taking me back to my hotel?"

"Don't worry where we are taking you. The *Commandante* and your American agent will decide what to do with you," said Jefe.

We slowly drove out of the airport. Thirty minutes later we approached a large sign on the edge of the highway which read "*Campo Militar.*" A few hundred yards past the sign, the car turned down a narrow-paved road. Soon we reached a restricted area surrounded by wire fences. At the main gate, guards armed with M-16 rifles waved us through. We continued up a steady incline which ended on a hilltop. It was a picture postcard setting with a panoramic view of the distant harbor and ocean. The only jarring note was the barren like structure of the camp, chalky and weather-beaten, from years of exposure to the hot sun, wind, and rain.

The military camp was home to hundreds of soldiers. Many of them were on duty about the grounds or standing individually on guard. They were dressed in greenish-brown combat uniforms and hard hat helmets.

Jefe left the car and entered a barracks. He returned with soldiers led by an officer who seemed to be in charge. My door was opened and I was pulled out from the back seat, hands still handcuffed behind. He gestured me to follow him and I walked behind, escorted by half a dozen soldiers carrying M-16's.

The room was about twenty feet square with the floor and walls of concrete. A desk and chair by the entrance, the only furniture in the room. I was led to one corner of the room by the sergeant and one of the soldiers. My handcuffs were removed and I was told to sit on the floor.

The sergeant put a hand on his revolver.

"Do not move from this spot."

He ordered all of the soldiers out of the room, except one, standing with his rifle pointed at me.

"I need to make a call to let my family know I'm safe."

"We wait for the *Commandante*," the sergeant answered.

"How long?"

"Who knows?" he shrugged. "The *Commandante* is in the hills searching for marijuana. Until he comes back, we are responsible for you."

He went back to his desk and began shuffling through papers and marking maps. My body still ached from the beating I'd received and the cement floor added no comfort. I would observe for the time being and find out as much as I could about the camp and the security. I needed to figure a way escape, or at least to get word out so someone would know where I was. My eyes wandered from the sergeant and armed guard, to the open door and closed window. Soldiers walked by the door, occasionally stopping to say a few words about maneuvers in the hills. It was clear I was in some sort of operational center that pinpointed areas to be raided.

I sat in the corner for hours, moving only slightly to change position. My body ached from the beating, and the rock-hard floor offered little comfort. Playing it cool was a necessity, even though I was churning inside. The worst thing for me would be to be troublesome. I had few options and patience seemed the smartest at this time. It would give me time to scope out the camp and get to know some of the soldiers. Money would probably be my strongest weapon, but I had to find the right time and place to dangle the prospect. I shifted my position again. Nobody paid attention.

Boldly, I stood up and stretched my arms.

My guard quickly pointed his rifle at me. "What are you doing?"

"Nothing. I'm getting stiff. Just want to stretch. Any chance of going for a short walk to get my circulation going?"

"You go nowhere without permission!"

"What about permission to use the toilet?"

"Sit down and I'll ask." He walked over to the sergeant.

He waved for me to come as the sergeant yelled instructions to the soldiers outside the room. I walked out with my guard right behind me. Eight soldiers joined us, four on each side. They escorted me to the latrine, M-16's in hand. This is insane, I thought. They must think I'm either a big kingpin or a mass murderer. I looked at the mesa on which we were encamped and noted how the brush-filled terrain sloped downward to a swamp-like place, green with plants. Surrounding it all, was what looked like miles of wire fence. If I found the right time to make my move, getting out of the camp would not be easy.

As I entered the latrine with my guard, the rest of the soldiers waited by the outside entrance. The stalls had no doors, and the toilets no seats. I was not permitted the luxury of privacy as the guard stood by the wash basin across from the toilet.

"You go there," he said pointing to the toilet.

A pile of old newspapers, obviously not for reading, were on the floor next to it. As I squatted, I watched him pull out what appeared to be a crudely rolled cigarette from his pocket and light it up. Finished, I moved towards to sink to wash my hands and noticed a familiar odor of marijuana coming from his cigarette. I looked at him and smiled.

"Aren't you afraid to smoke that around here?"

"I earned it. We burn tons of *mota* in the fields and they let us keep a little for ourselves. You want a hit?"

"No thanks, I'm here because of one of those *cigaros*. My name is Robert, they call me Roberto." I said, holding out my hand.

"I'm Ignacio, call me Nacho," he said as we shook hands. "Don't worry, for a little *mota,* you pay a small fine and are set free. You should not be here for something so small," he said taking another hit of his joint.

"I think they know they made a mistake and have to figure out what to do with me. The Federales said the *Commandante* and American agent will decide my fate. I keep being told to confess, but I didn't do anything."

"Doesn't matter. They want you to confess anyway. The *Commandante* has special ways to make you talk. First, you will feel like you are drowning, then they will go after your manhood. Very few can take the torture and not break. Better you save them the trouble and tell them what they want to hear."

"Why are you telling me this?"

"I have nothing against you. Soon my time in the army will be up and I'll go home. I'm a soldier, but we're not at war with you. The *Federales* choose to do their job. We don't. I may even go to your country for work, like my brothers did."

Nacho offered me some water from his canteen and walked me out. We returned to the main building surrounded by my escort of armed soldiers. He told me he would try get permission to bring me some food and something to drink.

By early evening, I was still confined my spot on the cement in the corner. A new sergeant had taken over the desk along with another replacement at the door. Nacho had brought me a bottle of coca cola and I was hoping he would make good on his offer to bring me some food. Several soldiers had been using the room as a rest stop during their breaks. Off duty, the soldiers made themselves comfortable, loosening their shirt collars and kicking off their shoes, while stretching out on the floor to swap stories or take a brief siesta.

My stomach was growling when Nacho returned just in time. Beans and tortillas had never tasted so good, and topped off with fresh *ranchero* cheese.

He began telling me about his family. His father was a fisherman who was injured in an accident at sea and was no longer able to work. His mother had a small business making meals for weddings and religious fiestas. He had two sisters, one married with two children, the other learning English and hoping to join her two brothers in the states. The money sent home by the brothers working in Los Angeles, had enabled them to buy a small house.

"I was raised near Los Angeles and my mother lives nearby. She always worries about me. Can you help me get word to her?"

He hesitated, thinking, "Maybe through my brothers, but I would need a phone number. Does she know you're in Mazatlán?"

"She knows it was my first stop before heading to San Miguel de Allende."

"We'll talk more tomorrow."

Nacho walked out and returned shortly with a blanket for me. I put it under my body to cushion the cold cement. I was still wearing the ripped shirt and long pants from the night before. Nacho stretched out with a half a dozen of his comrades to sleep.

With my first meal in over twenty-four hours, I thought that sleep would come quickly. It didn't. I knew I had little or no control over my fate. Everything was in the hands of this Mexican *Commandante* and an American agent, whoever he was. No friends or family had any idea where I was. I worried about what was coming next and how I would handle it. When my mind finally slowed down, I drifted off to sleep remembering Estela's last kiss.

Over the next few days the routine changed slightly. I was allowed to move from my corner when soldiers came to sweep the room. I visited the bathroom more than necessary just to get out. My guard escort was cut in half… two on each side. Several of the soldiers were smiling and speaking to me. Many of the them smoked marijuana openly. I was the first American they had ever seen at the camp. They wondered how terrible my crime must have been.

Nacho brought me food once a day, consisting of beans, tortillas, and cheese accompanied with a delicious hot drink, called *champurrado*. I savored every bite as my strength and spirits were improving.

Then came the news. The *Commandante* had returned. Nacho told me that his headquarters was located in a building which housed the Federal offices in downtown Mazatlán. I felt relatively safe in the barracks with the soldiers, but apprehensive about what might happen next. I had to try to get word out, so someone would know where I was. I reminded Nacho of his offer to have his brother contact my mother. I asked him to get me a pen and paper so I could write a letter to her.

After receiving permission from the sergeant, he returned with a pen, paper and an envelope. I wrote a brief summation of what had happened to me and where I was. I put Mom's name on the envelope with my cousin Bill's address. Hopefully Bill could handle this without worrying Mom. The sergeant had been staring my way as I was writing. As Nacho began to walk out with the letter, he was stopped at the desk and continued empty handed. The sergeant turned towards me with a smile and held up the envelope. Did that smile mean he would mail it? I had no idea.

I slept better that evening. Besides the letter, I had written Bill's phone number on a separate piece of paper for Nacho's brother in Los Angeles. One way or another, someone would know where I was. The atmosphere in the barracks had become more relaxed as some of the soldiers began to open up and talk to me. We taught each other expressions in our own language and had a few laughs at the mispronunciation of words. I was helping several with some conversational English, when a soldier burst into the room and began talking excitedly to the sergeant. He barked orders to the soldiers near me and they quickly followed him outside.

The sergeant returned, followed by two *Federales*. The younger one, neatly dressed with a Pancho Villa mustache, handed papers to the sergeant--while his older, slightly balding partner stared at me intently, while inhaling a cigar. Without a word they approached, ordered me up, and clamped handcuffs on me. As we walked out the door, Nacho was waiting. Our eyes met and I could tell he did not approve. I smiled and moved my lips…*gracias.* Soldiers were clustered around a pickup truck with government plates that would take me to my next destination. The door was opened and I was sandwiched in the middle of the two *Federales.*

"Where are you taking me now?"

"You are going to meet the *Commandante*," said the bald one.

"Good! Now I can show him there's been a big mistake."

Unlike the previous *Federales,* these two were talkative. For openers, I was offered a kilo of cocaine, "very cheap," as they put it. I told them I didn't need the cocaine, but could get them plenty of money, if I were to be set free. They seemed disappointed I didn't bite on the cocaine and began to tell me about the *Commandante.* I was warned to be ready to tell him everything. They detailed his sure-fire methods of making prisoners confess. If they were trying to soften me up, it wasn't working. I had already experienced the *chicharra* and heard the stories about what might come next.

We parked downtown in front of the Federal Building. The same American I had seen at the airport in the Ford Galaxy was waiting in front with Jefe, as my balding escort left the car to join them. The conversation became animated with hand gestures and glances in our direction. Then he hurried back to the car.

"*La Caja Caliente. Rapido!*" he told the driver to head to the Hot Box.

"What's going on? Are you going to let me go?"

"The *Commandante* will see you later. We have bigger fish to fry."

They parked the car near the Plaza in the center of town. It was brimming with families, squealing children, and single people who had come to stroll through the umbrella-like trees or relax on the cool grass. I had visited this historic square twice before on earlier trips. The first time to people-watch and have my shoes shined by an old timer full of interesting stories; a hero to his younger competitors. I had sampled tacos and tostadas at the small restaurant nearby.

The second visit was with Estela who offered a guided tour of the *Centro de Mazatlán*. We wandered leisurely arm in arm, passing through the central market with its fresh fruits and vegetables while savoring the aroma of authentic Mexican foods cooking in large pots. Clothing and souvenirs were sold to tourists from the many stalls inside. We continued walking and soon reached the historical Cathedral built in the 1800's. Finally, we ended up in the Plaza listening to music together on a bench under a tall shade tree. Neither of us had paid any attention to the old jail across the street.

Since leaving the Federal Building, I had pleaded, demanded, even attempted to bribe the *Federales* to let me call friends for help. My words seemed to have landed on deaf ears. Entering the Plaza, we slowed to a less conspicuous pace. I felt the grip ease on my arms. Suddenly, I was walking freely on my own.

"Don't talk or make any quick moves," the younger one advised me. I felt the tip of his revolver pushing hard into my ribs.

We passed a shoeshine boy, busy with a customer at his stand. Children romped around us. Here and there, lovers embraced under the trees in their own private world. I saw the spot where Estela and I had held one another. Was that memory really part of the past, or just my imagination?

It would have been easy to push one Fed into the other, as Felix had done. Easy, but not smart. I would have accomplished nothing more than frightening a lot of good people. As much as I wanted to escape, I wasn't going to risk getting innocent bystanders hurt. I had no doubt my captors would not hesitate to draw their guns and start firing. I remembered Jefe's reaction to Felix running away.

# 4

## *The Hot Box*

The building housing the central jail and police station looked as though it had been built years ago and somehow had survived the elements that came with age. Two stories high, it spread around a full city block. Once inside the fortress-like walls, however, its true size was apparent. Within the structure was a massive courtyard encompassing perhaps fifty percent of the facility's total space. Cluttered with wind-swept debris, this open-air area looked like a forsaken waste.

I was taken to a counter in an anteroom and met by an older man wearing police blues. I took him to be the jailer for he sported, besides the customary revolver, a large metal ring that held a number of keys. The *Federales* wasted no time in getting him aside to tell him things obviously not meant for my ears. More game playing. I turned my back and showed no interest.

The two *Federales* departed quickly, leaving me in the custody of my new keeper. I expected to be booked with some formality to make my imprisonment official. But no forms were filled out, no fingerprints were taken, no photo. He didn't even ask my name. He only asked if I had money to buy food and sodas.

"Not one peso," I told him, "but if I can use the phone, there will be plenty for that. And more."

"No," he said quickly, "you are under Federal control, "*Incommunicado*." With that he showed me into a short passageway toward a bolted door, the entrance to *La Caja Caliente*.

The "hot box" was a putrid hole. Wall-to-wall gray cement, no windows or ventilation. It was less than half the size of the quarters at the military camp. A concrete coffin. The air, stifling and rank, heavy with the odor of stale urine, was hot and humid.

"You piss here," the old man said, pointing to a rusty tin can, three-quarters full. God knows how many days it had been there. "If you want to crap, call a guard."

He uncuffed me and left quickly, clanging the heavy metal door behind him. Jutting out from one wall was a badly stained concrete slab for sitting. I sat there, feeling the perspiration run down my body. Alone in this small cell, my emotions began to take over. Questions, nothing but questions. How long would I be here? What are they going to do? Would I ever get out of this mess? How?

I felt a crushing pressure deep in my chest, an aching in my heart. Memories floated through my mind. It was as though I had been betrayed by someone who was very dear to me. My infatuation with Mexico encompassed the whole culture: the language and music; the festive spirit and the slower more enjoyable pace of life; the romanticism and tight bond of family. Most important were the special people I had met. This was my fifth trip into Mexico and I continued to learn more about its heart and soul. Each time I left reluctantly, with a yearning to return.

I pictured my friend Felix, the young hip waiter who taught me so much about his people and the language; laughing with me as I mispronounced the slang. Jose, the cab driver, who had invited me into his home for dinner, introduced his wife, and honored me as a friend. I wanted to walk through the walls, to pretend this had all been a bad dream—or to go back in time before I heard Ron Warren pounding on my hotel door.

I looked for meaning in what I had just experienced. Was it necessary to see the worst of Mexico to get a true perspective? Would I come out of this nightmare a better man and more aware human being? I had no idea how long I'd daydreamed. Maybe only minutes. In the sweat tank it was impossible to tell when day ended and darkness began. My sun and moon, a caged lightbulb no brighter than forty watts that burned constantly from a perch in the ceiling. The only clues to time were sounds outside my door. I soon came to know the voices of the guards and when the shifts changed. From the courtyard, I could hear the ritual of *lista*- the police roll call.

Hunger pains rumbled through my stomach. How good a tortilla and a scoop of beans would taste now. Every thought ultimately turned to food, friends, or home—subjects too painful to pursue. I stood over the tin can to urinate, unable to release a drop. Whatever liquid I had left in me was surely siphoning out through my pores. My clothes felt like a load of wet laundry against my skin. I removed my sweat-soaked shirt and laid it neatly on the slab, smoothing out the wrinkles. Heaven knows why.

I moved toward the doorway, taking tiny deliberate steps to make the trip seem longer. Then back to the slab. I did it again. And again. I crossed the room over a dozen times, blocking out the surroundings by concentrating on the precise movement of my feet. I went down and did pushups until I could do no more. I would stay strong. Soon, the ritual became hypnotic and I began to hallucinate. A man's face floated in and out of my thoughts, his features at first indistinguishable. With each appearance I strained to see more, damning him for being so elusive. It was like walking through a dense night fog, without lights, knowing something was ahead but unsure of what. I walked faster, and for a brief second, he stood before me. A shaft of light through the haze caught the line of a scar on his left cheek. No mistaking the man now. It was Jefe, and he had been at the Capri the night before I was arrested. The clicking sound of his shoe came back to me. He must have seen Ron on stage. What was really going on?

Loud voices in the corridor interrupted my thoughts. I knew hours had passed and it had to be late at night. A young man was shoved into the cell with me. Neatly dressed, he was extremely nervous and seemed to be in pain. With his unbuttoned shirt, I could see his nipples were raw and ringed with ugly welts. Pus was beginning to ooze from the dime-sized spots where a burning cigar had scorched his skin.

"I'm Roberto, I told him. Looking at you, I think we already have something in common."

"I'm Jorge." We shook hands and began to tell our stories.

He talked of a robbery at the beer plant where he was foreman. Despite a clean record, he was held responsible for the theft. "*Víctima propiciatoria*," he called himself. A scapegoat. There had been a confrontation with his supervisors. The *Judiciales* (State Police) were called in. A confession was prepared and set before him. He refused to sign it and was handcuffed and beaten. In the dim light of the hot box, Jorge took off his shirt and threw it aside.

I described my experience with the *Federales* and the joint they supposedly found. I recounted the stories I'd been told, and the days I had waited to be called before the *Commandante* and his persuaders.

"Marijuana has been used in my country for years by our ancestors for pain. My grandmother, Minga, made a liquid she would rub on to sore muscles for arthritis. You have nothing to fear," he said. "One *cigaro* is nothing."

Asleep, we were awakened by the sound of the door opening and the sounds of people yelling. We sat up just in time to see a large group of drunks being herded into our small space. These pitiful people picked up throughout the town, were brought into the hot box to sweat it out. There was hardly room for everyone.

The men stumbled and fought for places to stand or sit. Many had lost all control, retching and pissing at will. Jorge and I crouched on the cement bench, trying to be as inconspicuous as possible.

By morning *lista*, the intruders were gone, leaving the floor a pool of human waste and cigarette butts. If the smell was foul during their brief stay, it was incredibly worse as the sun rose and the temperature began to build. By mid-morning, no one had come to wash down the room; the combination of heat and stench, plus the sight of the mess, was unbearable.

"They don't care how we live," Jorge said. "If we're to survive, we must help ourselves."

But how? We had nothing but the tin can to use as a scoop. When Jorge insisted that we ask the jailer for a mop and pail, I looked at him in disbelief.

"They won't even give us drinking water. You think they'll bring us some for the floor?"

Jorge shrugged, "Who knows what goes on inside their heads."

Surprisingly, our request was granted, and we were also given water to drink. With a mop, broom, and soapy water we were able to clean up our temporary home and make it livable again. We had time to kill, and I wanted to pick his brain about the Mexican justice system.

"How do things work here? In my country after being arrested you are soon charged or let go and released on bail to wait for a court date. Supposedly, you are presumed innocent until proven guilty."

"It's much different in Mexico, Roberto. Here you are guilty until proven innocent. There is no formal court or jury. You and your attorney go to the judge's office and he decides your fate. There are rules of law that are not always followed. If someone has money, they pay and go free."

"Both of our countries have that in common," I told him.

Early that evening I heard a noise at the door. The old jailer stood squinting through the bars of the peephole. When he stepped aside, a young Mexican woman appeared in his place.

"Jorge?" she called softly.

Jorge had been drifting in and out of sleep and at first didn't notice. But her familiar voice reached him. He sat up slowly.

"Conchita," he cried, getting to his feet. For a moment, he forgot his aches. He hurried to touch her.

"The *Judiciales* came tonight," she whispered. "They searched everywhere. The drawers, the cupboards, the closets, under the bed."

"They found nothing, of course."

"I'm so frightened, Jorge. They said you did it."

"They lie, I'm innocent."

"I know, I know. But if you sign the papers . . ."

"Never! I didn't do anything."

Jorge reached through the bars and cupped her face in his hands. "Don't worry, *mi amor*. I'm coming home soon."

Conchita stared hopefully at her husband, her eyes filling with tears. "I've brought you food," she said, forcing a smile. She passed a paper bag through the opening. A moment later, the jailer returned and her visit was over.

Jorge hobbled back to the slab, holding the bag high. "Food," he grinned. "For us!"

More than two days had passed since I had seen food; a six-course meal at Chasen's couldn't have tasted better. Conchita had packed fresh fruit, wedges of cheese and a delicious chicken and vegetable mixture that we put inside tortillas.

It didn't take long to empty the bag. "I'm sorry there was so little," Jorge apologized.

"There was plenty. Thanks for sharing it with me."

Jorge waved off my remark. "Next time there will be more."

"Next time," I vowed, "we'll be free. We'll celebrate at the best place in town . . . you, Conchita, and me. My treat." As improbable as the invitation sounded, we shook on it.

I had put off visiting the jail's community toilet as long as possible. Since I hadn't eaten, I really didn't have the urge. Now I couldn't wait any longer. A guard led me from the hot box, down the main corridor, and out into the courtyard. The night air was like fresh flowers, soft and clean against my skin. Then he opened a door and stagnant sewer smells, decay and rot, wrapped around me once more. And the flies!

As I hovered above the cruddy hole with a bucket of water next to it, I was careful not to touch anything. I became preoccupied with a series of windows, just large enough for a man to slip through. They were barred, but the bars looked spindlier than those on our cell door. With the proper tools, I knew I could cut through those slivers of steel.

I mentioned my discovery to Jorge. "Yes," he agreed, "it may be the perfect way out. The room is isolated and on the ground floor. Once you are out the window, you can become lost in the street traffic. I'll talk to Conchita. She will bring what you need."

I appreciated his offer, but the more I thought about it, I doubted it would work. Cutting through the bars would make noise and take time. And the guard would be waiting by the door for me to finish my call of nature.

Again, Jorge was taken from the cell and I was left alone. What seemed like hours went by and I could barely hear screams of agony of someone being tortured. Was it, Jorge? I began to feel a queasiness in my stomach, wondering again what was in store for me, and how I would get out of the fix I was in.

About an hour later I heard footsteps outside my cell. Two guards were dragging Jorge to the entrance. His head was bowed and he stood upright only with the help of the guards. When they released him, his knees gave way. A boot positioned in the small of his back kept him from falling backwards and I caught him as he fell forward into the cell. I lifted him onto the slab and folded my shirt to lie his head on. His eyes were closed.

"It's OK now, it's me," I said, as he slowly opened his eyes.

Recognizing me, he said, "I almost signed it, Roberto. "They took me to a room across the courtyard with a very bright light. The one in charge wore dark glasses. He just gave orders and smiled. They brought the *chicharra* and…."

"You get some rest," I said, remembering the pain of the *chicharra*.

He read my eyes and said "You have to face fear to be brave,"

I just nodded and walked to my corner, curled into my ball, closed my eyes, and tried to empty my mind.

When I woke up to a new day, the cell was clean. No drunk visitors had arrived. Just myself and Jorge. The weekend must be over, I thought.

A few hours later Conchita was back with breakfast of *huevos a la Mexicana*, scrambled eggs with tomato, onion, and *chile*—I was in heaven. Jorge didn't tell her what he had gone through that night. He asked her about the children and told her to be strong. He made a point of being positive, so she wouldn't worry. Just seeing each other seemed to lift both their spirits.

Conchita had been the only outsider to visit us during the first few days of our confinement. Later that day the jailer came and brought me to a small room down the hall. A short chubby man, wearing a fancy long white Mexican shirt with slacks, was sitting at the table.

"Robert Miller?" he inquired.

"That's me," I said. "What can I do for you?"

"Ay, *señor* Miller, it's not what you can do for me, it's what I can do for you. I understand the charges against you and am here to help. I am *Licenciado* Eduardo Monterrubio," he stated proudly as he handed me his card.

"I am an attorney and have the best connections in Mazatlán which I have used for other Americans in your same circumstance." he continued.

"How did you find me? I was told I'm incommunicado and no one can know my whereabouts."

"As I told you, I have connections, very high connections, and am the finest attorney. Now do you want to be free, or keep asking questions," he said impatiently.

"Continue," I said.

He told me he would need my account of the arrest and not to leave out any details. He would also need the names of people who would vouch for me in Mazatlán. Lastly, he would need to know how he was going to get paid and the name of a family member or friend who would help me. He unzipped his portfolio and pulled out a notebook and pen.

Go ahead, I am ready," he said.

There was something about him I didn't like. He seemed arrogant and insincere. I can't trust this guy, but what choices did I have? This was a chance, at least, to let someone know where I was.

I began with Ron Warren, the Safari, and the rental papers left in my room. I described the Mauna Loa confrontation with the Feds, the hassling of my friends, and eventual search of my room. As I described the beating and torture I had endured, he seemed uncomfortable, asking me to hurry up and not even taking notes. When I mentioned the Military Camp, he stopped me, saying that he had heard enough.

"Give me the names and addresses of people in town who can vouch for you."

Felix would have been my first choice. We had spent time together and shared our thoughts and dreams with each other. Not being sure what happened to him after his escape from the Feds, I didn't want to risk giving his information to someone I didn't know, or trust. Later, I found out what a wise decision it was.

Jose, on the other hand would be perfect. I had met him the year before on my first trip to the area. He had lived in Los Angeles for fifteen years before buying a home in Mazatlán and becoming a taxi driver. He spoke good English and was a guide and interpreter to many visiting tourists. He had met both me and my cousin Bill on our first trip during *Semana Santa*. His friendliness was genuine and I had been invited to his house for a home cooked meal prepared by his wife, Rosa. I gave him Jose's name and told him where to find his taxi. At least someone I trusted would know where I was. He then handed me a blank piece of paper with an x near the bottom, and told me to sign it. I looked at him incredulously.

"You really think I'm stupid enough to sign a blank piece of paper. Fill in the top part, and then I'll decide whether to sign or not… after I read it."

"It will be your mistake not to trust me," he said, picking up the paper…disappointed. "Now tell me, who do I contact for the money."

"How much money are we talking about, and is this to pay a fine, or what?

"Only eight thousand pesos and I can work miracles" he responded. "It is for the *palanca*.

"*Palanca*, what's that?"

"Influence, connections, cutting through the red tape with the Federales, prosecutor, or judge. It's what I do best." he said.

"I get it. Everybody gets some money in their pocket and the case goes away. Now I understand, and I'm in. Just get me out of here," I told him.

I wrote down the phone number of my cousin Bill and his roommate Sean. They had both been to Mazatlán and would help without worrying Mom. At least now, I had a fighting chance.

I told Jorge about this attorney and his feeling was the same as mine. Didn't trust him and had never heard of him. He would have his wife talk to someone who might know something. He also thought eight thousand pesos was outrageous for one joint. That evening Conchita brought us another meal and sodas. This time with a surprise inside the food--a file.

"*Baño*!" I yelled as the jailer came to escort me to the shithole. I was anxious to see if the file would actually cut the bars. As I reached up to the bars and began working, the screeching of metal against metal was so loud I had to wait for outside noises to muffle the sound. I could tell this was not going to be easy and would take many more visits to complete the task. Probably more time than I had.

The next morning the jailer banged on our door with the butt of his gun. Monterrubio stood outside looking through the bars.

"I have good news," he said, smiling. He had reached my cousin Bill and explained my circumstances. Bill had told him someone would arrive tomorrow with whatever money they could round up. "He is not sure if he can get all eight thousand dollars that quickly."

"What do you mean eight thousand dollars? You said pesos. You set the price yourself."

"A slip of the tongue. But what is the difference, if your life is at stake."

"My life is at stake now and I haven't even been charged with a crime? C'mon!"

"Things work differently here in Mexico than in your country, but they do work when I am in charge. I will call him back and find out what he can come up with, so I can make a deal."

"I must see him before you receive one cent."

"Of course, do not worry, I will take care of everything," and waved as he scuttled away.

After he left, I didn't know what to think. Even though I trusted him even less now, there was hope that I would see someone from home.

Later that day I heard a familiar voice and footsteps approaching. The jailer opened the cell door and escorted me to the small room where I saw the person matching the voice. Jose rose to give me an *abrazo* (hug).

"I just found out you were here. "What's going on?"

"It's been one hell of a ride, but hopefully it's almost over."

I gave him the short version of what had happened to me and asked him to get word out to Felix and Estela. He told me that the Feds had come to his taxi stand and brought him in for questioning. They had interrogated him for hours and asked many questions about me and someone named Ron, then finally let him go. On the way back to his taxi he had found out from the driver where I was being held. Someone in Rosa's family had connections and was able to get him in for a visit. I gave Monterrubio's name to Jose and let him know who was responsible for the interrogation with the Feds.

"I'll check him out and keep an eye on you. Don't worry my friend, you're not alone anymore."

I felt relief. A good man and friend, who cared. Things were looking up.

# 5

## *Mordida*

Monterrubio showed up late the next morning. He was exuberant with the news that Sean would be arriving. I would be transferred out of the Hot Box and be able to see him on the way to my next temporary residence. There I would see the sky again and be in the open air with the sun and the stars. Sounded like he was making a commercial for a tourist resort. What really stoked me, was news of Sean's arrival and time for—"Let's make a Deal".

Early evening, the butt of the jailer's gun once again banged against our cell door. It was time for me to leave. I looked back at Jorge who moved toward me to give an *abrazo*.

"*Buena suerte, amigo*." I wished him good luck.

"*Vaya con Dios*, Roberto," he replied, as our eyes locked.

Standing behind the jailer were the two Feds that had transferred me from the *Campo Militar* and had offered me the cocaine. We moved quickly out the front entrance of the jail and into a Chevy Nova with no license plates and an official government sticker on the windshield.

"Where are we going," I asked. "Did my friend arrive?"

They weren't so talkative this time.

"Relax *señor*, and enjoy your freedom on this beautiful night."

After fifteen minutes, the car began to slow. Ahead I spotted the bright sign of a restaurant, Los Comales. In front, two men were standing as if they were waiting for someone. I perked up when I saw the bright red hair of the taller one. I'd know that "carrot top" anywhere. It was Sean, and he was with Monterrubio.

Sean Ryan was my cousin Bill's roommate and one of the most interesting characters I had ever met. His intelligence was off the charts and he had surprised me time and time again. Once he picked up my guitar and played a great flamenco rendition of "Manitas de Plata," as he told me about his travels with the gypsies in Europe. Another time we were in a hospital lobby with a baby grand piano when he sat and played Chopin, effortlessly. He and Bill had been leaders on competitive debate teams in high school and both had won competitions. To listen to them take a subject to places I never imagined after sharing a joint, was mesmerizing. They fed off each other and could have had their own show. He was a talented poet and his heart was with his fellow Irishmen.

As the car pulled to a stop, Sean walked over and opened the door. He slid in the back seat beside me.

"Well—it's a fine mess ya got yerself into this time, lad."

"Crazy Irishman! I hope you're up to the challenge," I told him.

The car door slammed shut. We pulled away, leaving Monterrubio behind.

"You're looking relaxed and well-fed," I said.

Sean grinned. "You don't look half bad yerself—even with whiskers. But, ah ... well, they say even your best friends won't tell you."

"What's wrong?"

"Your deodorant's dead."

"Can't be me," I said. "I've already had my shower this month."

"Sorry," Sean nodded to the front seat, "must be your chauffeur and valet."

Our companions up front seemed uninterested in our conversation. Sean laughed, then moved in closer and lowered his voice.

"Where'd you find this Monterrubio?"

"I didn't, he found me. I don't trust him."

"Says you'll be out in a few days."

"Right," I gave a questioning look. "Did you bring the money?"

"Yep."

"Did you give it to him?"

"No, I told him I had to see you first."

"Don't give it to him until you check him out with the American Consulate and anybody else that might have a line on him."

"That might be rough."

"Why?"

"As soon as we're through talking, they're taking me back to meet with him. He knows I have the money."

"Stall him if you can!"

"All right," he promised. "Now, what about you?" The sparkle was gone from his eyes.

"What do you mean?"

"I brought some extra cash." He reached into his pocket and pulled out a neatly folded packet of bills.

"That could make things easier," I said.

He slipped the money into my palm. For the first time in days I had some sense of security.

Sean nudged me. "Hide it," he whispered.

This was no time for daydreaming. I started for my pants pocket, then stopped. The shirt pocket was out too. I slowly reached down and took off my left shoe. Then I wadded the money into my sock, under my arch.

Our escort upfront turned his head towards us. "What's wrong, you run out of talk?"

"Extra sensory perception," Sean told him. "Communication

through thought transference. Very big in the States." Leave it to an Irish poet for that bit of malarkey.

"What about Mom?" I asked hurriedly, pulling on my shoe. "Did you tell her?"

"Bill and I talked it over. You'll be out soon, so why lay this on her now?"

"Good. Don't want her to have a clue. She worries a lot."

"She thinks you're getting ready to start your archaeology class.," Sean said.

"Yeah—I should be on my way to the Institute now."

"Next year," Sean smiled.

"Next year," I repeated, half-heartedly.

The car turned off the paved highway onto a rough dirt road leading through Colonia Juárez, one of the poorer sections of town. The houses grew progressively smaller, more ramshackle. "Where are we heading?" Sean asked.

I looked at him strangely. "Didn't Monterrubio tell you?"

"Only that he wanted us to have some time together."

"They're taking me to a prison. Like a resort they say, where I can relax under the stars and beautiful sky." We laughed together at my attempted humor.

# 6

## *Prison*

Cárcel Público Municipal (CPM) had a look of decay. Even the dim light of evening couldn't mask its scars. Built many years earlier as temporary quarters to house prisoners, it was condemned by local officials in 1972. But instead of being closed, it was re-classified from a state and local jail, to a federal prison.

Now it contained five sections. "*Considerados,*" for political prisoners who had committed crimes against the government. "*Grande,*" the largest section, was divided into separate areas for men and women. It boasted a small restaurant, exercise yard, volleyball court and was supposedly for prisoners who had been sentenced. "*Separos,*" the smallest, was the punishment section and isolation ward for the most violent and mentally ill. "*Mujeres,*" the women's section. And "*Correccionales,*" for those still awaiting sentencing.

Before the car came to a complete stop, four men in uniforms and carrying M-16 rifles surrounded us. Sean took my arm.

"If you have to get in touch with me, I'll be staying at the Az-teca Inn."

"I'll remember," I said.

Then he pulled off his shirt, a short-sleeve Hawaiian print. "Take this," he said. "It's clean and believe me, you need it. You'll definitely make a better first impression."

"What about you?"

"I'll stop by the hotel to get another one and try to delay seeing Monterrubio until I check with the consulate.

Sean didn't smile this time. "Take care. I'll see you tomorrow."

The four guards led me inside the main building through a waiting area, down a passageway past a barred door, and into a large room with a desk and typewriters. Only one person was on duty. While he was writing down information on assorted forms, my eyes wandered. I saw a group of prisoners behind a caged door. Beyond them, a long corridor. On the other side, there were several more doors and benches lined outside one wall. Signs indicated this was reserved as a meeting area for inmates, their attorneys, and visitors. Next to a gun rack, near the counter, was a framed picture of Mexico's patron saint "La Virgen de Guadalupe". I looked at her image—brown skin and black hair with an angel at her feet, encircled by rays of sunlight.

An armed man with keys appeared and took me down the long corridor while another followed behind. Near the end we came to a crossroad and turned to the right. Not much farther we stopped and my handcuffs were removed. The guard unlocked a heavy barred door.

Two prisoners stood ready to meet me. One was on duty, part of a round-the-clock watch. The other said his name was Chico, an interpreter. Both were members of the "Commission", the governing body which enforced the law of the prison from within; inmates who ruled with the approval and backing of the warden. Chico led me inside, babbling in pitiful English as we went. He was a Cuban refugee who had spent some time in the United States before moving to Mexico where he was busted on a narcotics charge. If he wasn't an addict on the outside, he had since become one.

"Welcome to Correccionales. I am Chico and will help get what you need," he said. "We talk more after you see Mudo."

We were in an open courtyard, about sixty feet square, surrounded by high brick walls. The ground was littered with scores of bodies standing or lying on bare concrete and rickety cots, some occupied and others vacant. Low voltage light bulbs burned here and there casting eerie shadows as people shuffled about, on their way to nowhere. I had suddenly become a character in a Fellini movie.

We stopped before a makeshift door, one of a series of huts, called *carracas*, that butted against the far wall. These temporary homes were made from scraps of lumber and cardboard, while corrugated metal roofing covered the tops. Chico briefed me for the upcoming indoctrination.

"Mudo have much power. Very rich. *Presidente* of the Commission." He talked quickly, nervously, telling me to listen attentively whenever Mudo spoke and to wait for his translation.

"There's no need for that," I told him. "I understand Spanish and speak some."

"No, no, no," he shot back, "no good. Ees my job--I talk first. You wait for me to say in English."

I had the feeling his job was in jeopardy. Chico knocked timidly on the door then peeked inside. "OK," he said and we entered.

The *carraca* was furnished sparsely, but comfortably. A large television set in one corner, a small refrigerator in another. Various trinkets, necklaces, rings and other valuables were stashed in piles on the floor and on a long makeshift shelf which also held a cassette player and a fan. A bed, partially hidden by a blanket slung over a rope, was occupied by a scantily clad brown skinned girl and a brawny man in shorts and sandals. They were watching the tube. Seeing us, the man turned down the sound and snapped open a can of beer.

"Mudo," Chico muttered to me, then dropped his head in a subservient bow.

Mudo stood about five feet nine. He was probably in his early thirties. He had the slicked back hair and the cool style of a pachuco. Despite the hour and relative darkness inside his *carraca*, he wore sunglasses. It was impossible to tell where he was looking or what he was thinking.

He stood for a minute staring in my direction then took several gulps of beer and belched. He grabbed the blanket and yanked it across the rope, cutting off all view of the girl. "Roberto Miller?" he asked finally.

Chico nodded and I answered yes.

"*Qué traes?*"

"You bring something with you?" Chico translated.

I started to say no then held up Sean's shirt which I still carried.

"*Es todo . . . no más?*" Mudo asked.

"Is all ... no more?" Chico translated

I held up the shirt again. "This is all."

Mudo reached for the shirt and I handed it to him. He squeezed it from hem to collar, then checked the seams. "*Dónde están sus joyas?*"

"Where is your jewelry?"

"The *Federales* took everything. My money, my ring, my identification, everything."

Chico translated my words into Spanish.

"*No dinero?*"

"No money?"

I stuffed my hands into my pockets and pulled the cloth inside out. "No money."

"*Tiene reloj?*"

"You have watch?"

"I had one, but the *Federales* took it from me."

Chico translated.

"*Anillos?*"

"Rings?"

"Nope,"

Chico looked patronizingly at the commission leader, then at me.

"Don't say no if you mean yes. Mudo very good man. Very honest. He have many rings and money from many prisoners. He not keep them. Just hold for you so don't get stolen. Mudo not want this to happen. He only ..."

Mudo cut Chico's lecture short. "*Callate!*" he told. him. "*Hablas mucho.*"

Chico moved back a step and lowered his eyes after being told to shut up.

"*Ahora,*" Mudo continued. "*Veremos si dices la verdad.*"

Mudo apparently did not buy the answers I had given him. Now he would get to the truth…. "*Quítate la ropa!*"

"Take off your clothes!" Chico commanded, mocking his leader.

I just stared and then thought, what the hell?

"My pleasure," I responded.

Off came the ripped smelly shirt. Then my wrinkled pants. I stood in my underwear, shoes and socks.

Chico gathered the dirty clothes and began to check through them. Mudo snapped his fingers for me to continue.

"*Zapatos!*"

Without thinking, I kicked my "shoes" towards Mudo. Chico was too involved in his explorations to translate. I pulled down the top of my left sock and started for my right sock, hoping my eagerness would convince Mudo I had nothing to hide. Then I felt the file. He would not be interested in it, I knew, but seeing it might spark an interest below the sock.

"*Hay nada aquí,*" Chico said he found nothing in my discarded items.

Mudo finishing checking my shoes held out his hands and took the clothes from Chico. He sighed, obviously becoming bored.

*"Díle los lujos que tenemos aqui."*

While Mudo double checked my clothes, fingering every inch of material, Chico informed me of the many comforts available to a prisoner at CPM. I learned that I could buy a *carraca* of my own—for five thousand pesos. And a cot to sleep on for three hundred pesos. Chico would even help find me an unused spot, for a small tip. Otherwise, I'd have to sleep on the concrete. I also learned that use of the toilet, shower, or telephone cost money.

"You pay two hundred pesos now or clean toilets in the morning," Chico said.

"I have no money," I reminded him.

Mudo continued searching my old clothes and mumbled something about money from home.

"You get money from *familia* and friends?" Chico asked.

"Sure," I said, "from California."

He turned to Mudo, looking for a signal. Mudo nodded, then laid back on his bed with the *señorita*.

From then on everything was go. Whatever I wanted was mine on credit; I only had to ask. Of course, there was a hitch; I would see little of the money when it arrived. I put my clothes back on, including the Hawaiian shirt Sean had given me.

Later, when we stood outside Mudo's carraca, Chico kept trying to convince me to buy something. He could get me a small package of grass for "only" twenty pesos. Or he could furnish me with a small "fix" of heroin for the same price. A joint or a fix, he promised, would help get me through my first night in *Correccionales*.

"Mudo give you credit. Ees good. You relax, not think you here. *Mañana*, you feel better. Chico knows."

I wasn't nervous or upset, just tired. Really tired. All I wanted was a place to lie down. A few minutes later Chico and I stood next to an empty cot.

"Mick ees Americano and he let you sleep on half his cot," Chico said. "You pay me later."

Chico brought the man over and introduced me, explaining that I had just arrived and was looking for a place to sleep for the night. Mick's eyes were glassy, like someone not quite in touch with reality. Looked like he had already taken some of the heroin I'd been offered.

"Line up a spot of your own," he said in a slurred voice. "My cot barely holds me." Then he dragged himself away.

Chico raised an eyebrow. "Mick strange person."

"Why's he here?"

"Here long time . . . and long-time more."

"Why?"

"Murder person. Kill taxi driver near beach."

I took a deep breath, grateful that I wasn't sharing this American's bed.

Chico yawned. "You want grass or sometheeng to make you feel good? Sell cheep."

I nodded in the negative and he scampered off.

After Chico left, I decided to wander around to check out the surroundings. Walking past different groups of inmates, I was barely able to see through the dim lights hung by strings in the dark night. I took in the improvised *carracas* made up from various materials that lined the exterior of the compound and provided privacy for the privileged. In the middle of the compound countless prisoners were outside and in the open. I passed bodies lying on the ground, squeezed between inmates stretched out on cots. Tired, yet tense, I would be careful in choosing my spot to lie down for the night. Mick was in for murder and I had no idea what crimes anyone else around me had committed. I finally picked a spot that looked safe in a space between two cots. My eyes met the owner of the cot on my left and I received a nod and a hand gesture offering me the space. I wadded my old shirt into a makeshift pillow and took one last look at the black sky full of bright shimmering stars. What a difference from the hot sweaty concrete box I had spent my previous nights in. I thought about Jorge and wondered how he was doing as I drifted off to sleep.

Just before daybreak I felt something brushing against my hair on the top of my head. Was I dreaming? Then I felt something crawling on my chest. I opened my eyes and could make out the shape—the long-pointed head, the spindly legs, and a whip-like tail. As I jumped up, the huge rat fell to the ground and scurried off. My adrenaline was flowing now and I was wide awake. Biggest rat I had ever seen.

"Leesta, Leesta, Leesta" was shouted out they pounded on the *carracas* and sleepy prisoners appeared outside in two distinctly separate lines, one for Federal prisoners and the other for State. Each name was called out loudly and the prisoner would respond and step forward. There were a number of American names in the Federal line.

"Ramirez."

"Si."

"Osuna."

"Aqui."

"Bloom."

"Yo."

"Dunn."

"Heeoh."

"Lopez."

"Presente."

More names were called and the early morning line slowly inched forward. As the newest arrival, my name was called last.

"Miller."

"Here."

I stepped forward and noticed many of the Americans staring at me. A young man wearing a t-shirt and shorts walked up to me with a friendly smile.

"I'm Cosey. You come in last night?"

"Yep, I was a late arrival." I told him.

"Come over to my humble abode and we can talk," he invited.

"Sounds good, maybe you can fill me in on this place."

I followed him to his "humble abode" which consisted of his cot and a fold up chair. We sat down and Cosey started by telling me his story. He was a twenty four-year old from Half Moon Bay, near San Francisco. He and his nineteen-year old girlfriend, Gretchen, were driving in their camper when they were detained at a roadblock south of Mazatlán. The Feds found bags of green herbal teas and money. They accused them of transporting marijuana and told them to sign a confession. When they refused, the electric cattle prod was brought out and Cosey was given a taste of it. They laughed maliciously about how it would be used to rape Gretchen. He wasted no time in signing the confession and was brought straight to *Correccionales,* while Gretchen was set free. She now lived near the prison, visiting and bringing food whenever she could.

When I told him about my journey from the night club and grassy field, to the military camp and hot box, before arriving at CPM, he was surprised.

"I haven't heard of anyone coming in through your route. That's really strange. Must be something more to it than just one joint."

"Strange is the least of it."

"Did you talk to the American consul," he asked.

"No, I was "incommunicado" and couldn't even make a phone call. Finally, an attorney showed up who must have been sent by the Feds. That's how I was transferred here."

"Who's the attorney?"

"Monterrubio", I answered.

"Wow…. unbelievable. You're the only one here that has the same attorney as me."

"What's he doing for you?" I asked.

"Not much. It all happened months ago and I'm still here. He says it's more difficult because I signed the confession. I know he's connected. He made a deal that worked for some other Americans."

"I don't trust him."

"Don't blame you," said Cosey. "Hard to know what to believe. I've been here for months and haven't even been found guilty of anything."

"It's been at least a week for me and I haven't seen anyone besides the Feds who beat the shit out of me, and some soldiers at the military camp. I don't even know if I have been charged with a crime."

He reached into his pocket and pulled out a sheet of paper.

"Listen to this- direct from the Mexican Constitution—'The accused may not be forced to be a witness against himself.' They conveniently forgot about this with me and Gretchen."

"How about this joke. 'Punishment by mutilation and infamy, branding, flogging, beating with sticks, torture of any kind-are prohibited.'"

I shook my head thinking about Jorge.

"Let's take a break and get some breakfast. I'll fill you in on *Correccionales.*"

With food in my stomach, I patiently listened to Cosey's rundown on my new home. Mudo ran *Correccionales* with the backing of some heavies in the drug trade of Mazatlán who had put up money and made arrangements with the warden. Profits from selling drugs and extortion went into the hands of Mudo, his backers, and the warden. Mudo's henchmen consisted of Gorilla, Pipino, and Nacho. They often carried clubs and knives to keep everything under control. Chico was the snitch and hustler, willing to do anything to earn money for his next fix. Everything cost money, from a place to sleep, use of the good toilet, food, making a phone call, and the extortion scams that would come up periodically. Mudo liked to give Americans a free sample of heroin when they were down. Eventually many of them became steady customers.

Visiting days were Thursdays and Sundays. Visitors were allowed to enter mornings; from nine to noon, and afternoons; from one to five. Each visitor was given a number printed on a wooden token, which was recorded and kept on file along with the person's name and local address. Everyone coming into the prison was frisked twice, once near the front door and again in a separate room. The searches were far from thorough (Cosey never heard of anyone being stripped at CPM) which made it relatively simple to smuggle in small items. Larger things were usually no problem either. Money or a gift, worked wonders.

*Correccionales* was overflowing with bodies on visiting day. Friends and relatives often seemed to be in a festive spirit while eating and drinking, despite the sordid surroundings. For those prisoners fortunate enough to have visitors, it was a time of jubilation. For the majority of Americans, so far from home and virtually alone, it was often depressing. There was little to do but wander about watching others with loved ones, while longing for their own who were far away. Of course, those with wives or girlfriends looked forward to this day. Anyone without a partner could arrange to have one brought over from the women's section, if they could afford it.

I felt a tap on my shoulder and low and behold, it was Chico.

"Get lost," said Cosey.

"You have *visita*," he said to me.

"Go ahead. Just follow him to the main entrance. There'll be a guard waiting to take you to the meeting room."

"Thanks for breakfast," I told him.

"When you get back, come see me. We'll have to get you some things."

At the end of the long corridor I could see a room with desks and typewriters. The night before the office had been unoccupied. Now it was crowded with people at work. Off in a corner, seated on a bench, Sean was waiting. He didn't look good.

"How'd you sleep?" he asked.

"OK—until a huge rat came by to wake me up," I answered. "What happened to you?"

"My head's going around in circles. I've been downing coffee all morning."

"Trouble sleeping?"

"That's not the half of it."

"Rats?"

"What?"

"Nothing," I said. "What's wrong?"

"Last night was a circus. My Irish blood was tested. I couldn't let those fools out drink me. Didn't sleep much, and my head feels like I hit it on the blarney stone."

"What happened?"

"Pancho and the other clown started to take me to meet Monterrubio and pay him the dough. I told them to hold their horses. I couldn't go back there without a shirt. Great way to stall and put it off, right. No chance. They came up to my room with me while I changed, then drove me over to meet with your friend."

"He's not my friend."

Sean went on to describe his unexpected evening. When they arrived at the restaurant, Monterrubio was waiting with another *Federale* with a long scar on his cheek. He took Sean's ID then made a phone call to give the info to someone on the other end. From the restaurant they all drove out to the Capri.

"Monterrubio was in command all the way. You should have seen him in action." Sean paused as if to make a point. "I'll tell you one thing," he said, his eyes narrowing, "He seems to be in pretty tight with the Feds."

"Be careful," I said. "The one with the scar busted me, and I'm almost positive I spotted him at the Capri the night I was with Ron. Something's not right. Why would he drag you to a place like that?"

"To impress me. To show me how easily he can handle the Feds. They're not going to file the charges, right? And I think he wanted to get laid. He took some lassie to her room out back. Then the one with the scar started talking to me about Ron, like I knew who he was. I told him I had no idea who he was talking about. He acted like he didn't believe me."

"What did you find out about Monterrubio?

"I called the Consulate and spoke to Vice Consul-Parker."

"And?"

"They vouch for him. No negative reports. He's on their recommended list. Parker didn't even know about you. Asked me questions and I got a little upset with him. I told him you were busted over a week ago, and how could the Consulate know nothing."

"What did he say?"

"Told me he's been frustrated by the lack of communication from the Mexicans. Said he would get on it immediately."

I sighed. "I talked to another Monterrubio client, right here. Says he retained him because he got a couple of guys off without trial. But he's been here six months…without a verdict."

Sean just shook his head. "I have to meet him in an hour. Needs the money this morning to pay the Feds. If not, it'll be too late… It's up to you."

I took a deep breath. "If the Feds aren't paid, I don't get out; but they could take the money and file anyway? Try to get something in writing."

The guard escorted me back to the yard and surprisingly, no Chico. Was my luck changing? I headed back to Cosey's cot and sat down to wait for him. Two cots down, a Mexican was strumming his guitar and singing "*Tristes Recuerdos*," a love song I had heard many times. Cosey arrived and waited for the song to end. He could tell I was really into it. Now he would tell me Enrique's story.

"His is a sad story. The bus he was riding in was stopped at a roadblock. Some grass was found in a suitcase in the baggage storage. With no one claiming it, The Feds picked Enrique out to take the rap."

"Another guilty til proven innocent."

"Here's the worst part. He came in here with two good legs. But if you want to know why those flies are buzzing around his cot, it's because they amputated one of his legs and it's inflamed and leaking pus. Good man with a big heart and has a lot of friends around here. Speaks only Spanish, so maybe you can get to know him better than I have."

"I'd like to get to know him--love the music."

"How's your money situation?" he asked. "You need to get lined up with a cot, unless you like sleeping on cement."

"Been sleeping on cement for a week and still don't like it. And the rats are huge. Don't want them messin with me again."

"Don't imagine you would," he laughed. "I might have a line on a cot for you."

"I'm all ears, but I want to ask you a question first. I don't feel comfortable showing big wads of cash around here. Just picked some up from my visitor. Any suggestions?"

"Definitely. If word gets out you have money, you won't be able to sleep. The hustlers and junkies'll be watching and waiting for a chance to pounce. Best thing is to give some to the store like most of us do. You'll have an open line of credit."

He went on to explain that Ramirez ran the bank in *Correcionales* for larger sums. He had been busted with two Texans, John and Barry, loading a plane with weed.

"He's trusted, connected, and has his own *carraca* with a cook and bodyguard."

"First thing for you to do is spend some of that on a cot and I think opportunity is coming our way." He was looking at a tall, light skinned black man.

"Here comes Sully, a junkie with soul. That's his cot next to us."

"Cosey, just the man I want to see. I'm hurtin bad. Need my medicine. Spot me ten pesos and you'll get back twenty."

"No thanks, Sully. I'd have to stand in line for a year to see it, but maybe my friend, Robert, can help you. He needs a cot and I heard yours is for sale."

"You crazy? Where'd you hear that?"

"The grapevine," Cosey answered.

Sully took a long look at me.

"Where you from?"

"Southern Cal, near LA," I told him.

He grinned at me.

"OK home. Bout time we got someone from where it's at. I'll give you a deal on my cot…. SoCal discount…only five hundred pesos."

Cosey almost choked on the soda he was drinking.

"Cut the crap, Sully. You want to charge him double because he's from your hometown? Take two hundred pesos and I'll talk him into it."

"No way Coz, I need at least three hundred to last the week"

"I can give you two fifty right now," I offered and started pulling pesos out of my pocket.

Sully's eyes followed the money. "You drive a hard bargain, homeboy."

I handed him the money and we shook hands. I had my cot and Sully had enough to get by for a while. I was now situated between Cosey and Enrique. At least I felt as though things were getting a little better for me, inside the walls. I just hoped Sean would come through and I would gladly give Sully his cot back.

The afternoon "*Lista*" was called and I was the last name in the Federal line again, but this time the Americans weren't so groggy and a couple of them stopped by to say hi.

"I'm Randy. You just get in? he said, offering his hand.

"Robert," I said, shaking it, "and you're right—just in."

Standing next to us was another American, a little older with long brown hair and a friendly demeanor.

"I'm Gary," he said as we shook hands.

'We have that *carraca* right in the middle," he said, pointing to it. "C'mon by later and meet the gang. We have a nightly poker game, if you're up for it."

Early that evening I peeked into the carraca. It was sparsely furnished with a bunk bed, a small table, and crates used as stools for the poker game. There were some personal pictures of Gary and Randy with girlfriends and family, a cassette player for the music, and graffiti, "Welcome to Nixon's Pawn Shop." The song, 'Hotel California', was playing in the background.

There were four players and the game had already started. Randy waved me in.

"Hey Rob, come on in."

"Welcome," said Gary. "This is John and Rich," introducing the two I hadn't met.

"Howdy partner, Long Horn John from Texas," he nodded to me as he picked up his cards.

"Greetings, Rich from New York," waving from across the table.

"You all got busted for drugs," I asked.

Innocent or guilty, that's what we're in for," said Gary. "Feds found a gram of coke and a spot of hash on me. Dumb bastards called it opium. They can't tell the difference."

Randy finished dealing the hand and lit up a joint. After taking a hit, he passed the joint to John.

"They got me on the ferryboat to La Paz sitting behind the wheel of my camper with five hundred kilos of Acapulco Gold." Randy continued.

"Damn."

"That ain't shit! My brother-in-law and I got busted with a planeload. Must have been close to a thousand kilos," John bragged. 'What are you in for?"

"A joint," I said.

"I'll take two cards," Rich said. "What was that Rob?"

"I'm charged with one joint."

All of the men looked at each other and burst out laughing.

"You're really big time then," John said. "Give me three cards. It don't matter what you're busted with, you get the same time as all of us. Five years, three months minimum. Did you confess?"

"Hell no! No way I'd confess to something I didn't do."

"Right on brother," said Randy.

"Survival is the name of the game here, said Rich. "Besides the head trips, there are diseases all over the place."

"What diseases?"

Tuberculosis, scabies, typhoid, and leprosy to name a few."

"Leprosy! Jesus Christ, what did I get myself into?"

"We're all in the same boat." said Randy. "You never know what these "*pendejos*" are up to. And they try every trick in the book to get more bread. "

I was able to hear all of their stories in more detail.

Randy was in his mid-twenties, a surfer from Newport Beach who looked every inch the part with his long blond hair and smooth, deep tan. He had been arrested on a ferryboat to La Paz sitting behind the wheel of a camper loaded with marijuana. Luckily his girlfriend Sue and their three-year old daughter, Ina, had boarded the ferry separately and were not picked up with him.

Gary, five years older than Randy, was part owner of a successful music publishing company in Hollywood. He had been arrested at a roadblock leading into Mazatlán when the Feds had found his personal stash of cocaine and hashish, which they mistakenly called opium.

John, twenty-eight years old, was from Texas where he had been a respected member of his community church and manager of the parts department for a Ford dealership. His brother-in-law, Barry, had invited him down to Mazatlán for a vacation and to help him out on a mission. Barry owned a computer company that was struggling to make ends meet. His creditors gave him a chance to recover all he owed and more by delivering the money and overseeing the loading of a plane with pot. Barry asked John to drive him to the ranch where they were busted loading the plane, along with Ramirez.

Rich hailed from New York where he ran his own paint contracting business. Tall, about six-feet two, he had curly brown hair, a beard, and wore glasses. Friendly, good natured and intelligent, he was proud of his Italian heritage. Like Randy, he had been arrested on the ferry to La Paz, but his stash had been hidden in the false bottom of a motorboat hitched to the back of his car. They knew exactly where to look. Someone had snitched him off.

I watched the game for a while longer then went out for a breath of fresh air and to think about everything. It was a quiet night in *Correccionales* and a new moon was coming out in the darkened sky. As I sat down on my cot, Enrique was playing guitar, just finishing a song. His eyes were so expressive, you could almost look into his soul.

"I'm Roberto," I told him and shook his hand.

"*Mucho gusto*," he continued in Spanish "I'm Enrique, but my friends call me Kike."

"You're new here. Where do you come from, Roberto?"

"I live near Los Angeles."

"Not too far from where I live with my son's family, in Tijuana."

"I can drive to Tijuana in less than three hours," I told him. "Coming back though I might spend two hours in line just waiting to cross."

Enrique laughed, "My son has told me the same thing. Sometimes he has to go to Los Angeles to pick up supplies for his company. He always wants to cross around four in the morning so the line won't be so long. He gets frustrated saying he's losing money, waiting so long."

"I love your music. How long have you been playing?"

"Since I was a child. My family farmed *tomatillos* and chile peppers in Los Mochis for many years, but one of my uncles was a great musician. I learned everything from him when I was very young. After work, I would listen to him play for hours. He taught me so much. From the first time I heard him play, I knew music would always be a part of my life."

"Listening to you, I think you were born to make music. I can feel it."

"We make passionate music with songs that tell stories about life."

"I know what you mean. Sometimes I don't understand all the

words, but I can feel it, in here," touching my heart. "I even learned the words to a couple of songs."

"Which songs have you learned?"

"*El Rey* and *Se Me Olvidó Otra Vez.*"

"Very passionate and popular songs. And you know all the words?"

"Definitely. After a few beers, I really get going."

Enrique began to play *El Rey* and invited me to sing along with him. Later, as he continued to play some soft ballads, I laid down on my cot, closed my eyes and thought of home.

My parents were divorced. Dad, happily remarried to Joyce, was often traveling around the world playing golf. Known as Nummie in the golf world, he played competitively against some of the best, including Ben Hogan and Sam Snead. He had offers to turn pro, but preferred to keep his construction company going. I had been brought up in a family of carpenters and helped Dad and my uncles build houses from the age of 14. While in high school and college I had enjoyed making a few extra bucks each summer working outside with my uncles. Lately, I had only seen Dad occasionally, when our schedules allowed it. We would meet for dinner and update each other on the latest. I wondered where he was now.

My mother, Barbara, worked as Deputy Court Clerk at the Beverly Hills Courthouse after transferring from Inglewood. In her late forties, her once black hair was now an honest silver. A together and independent lady, extremely warm and caring, she was never too busy to listen to my latest thoughts and questions. When I was considering going to law school, she took me back to meet the judge in his chambers. I would share my dreams of life and love of travel with her. She always made sure I would let her know where I was going and made me promise to write or send postcards. She was remarried, and I had become friends with her husband, Mike. I drifted off to sleep thinking of family and hoping the new day would bring good news.

The next afternoon Chico came by and beckoned me to follow him. I had a visitor. Monterrubio was waiting for me in the visitor's area, fidgeting with the lock on his briefcase. Sean was sitting across from him with a look of frustration on his face.

Sean rolled his eyes, "I think I'll let you hear it straight from the horse's mouth."

"We have a small problem," Monterrubio told me. His expression was grim.

"You got the money, didn't you?"

"Yes. But unfortunately, it arrived too late."

I stared at him. "What do you mean too late?"

"The money was for the Federal police, to pay them not to file charges."

"Yes."

He shrugged his shoulders. "The charges have been filed."

"But you said that if . . ."

"Do not worry," he cut in, a forced smile breaking on his face, "it is not so serious. There is another way."

I listened.

"We must go beyond the *Federales* and straight to the District Attorney. He will state there is not enough evidence to hold you."

"There isn't any evidence! Just what am I being charged with?"

"Things are looking much better. Before I spoke with the *Federales* you were charged with possession of marijuana and opium. Now you are only charged with possession of a small quantity of marijuana."

"This is unbelievable. I've never seen a paper that states I've been charged with anything."

"It has been filed," he said in a sure voice.

"This is a railroad," I told him.

"No mention has been made of your association with the person Ron, who my country wants very much. Your charges are minor."

"What about the D.A.? How long will it take to make the deal . . . and get me out of here?"

"Not long, do not worry. You have credit with me from the money I received, but there will be additional expenses."

He nibbled at his thumb then picked a speck of skin from his tongue. "Another twenty-five thousand pesos should be sufficient, and I can guarantee you will be set free."

I felt sick. "Impossible," I said. "There's no way we can come up with that much money."

"There are many fees. The District Attorney must be paid, many officials of his staff, there is my time, the . . ."

"Earn what you were already paid for."

He checked his watch. "Think of tomorrow, not today. The money is nothing. You are in a good position now, do not worry."

Don't worry? I questioned.

"You are not yet formally imprisoned. Only under arrest. But I will tell you this. Once your imprisonment is official, you will face a five-year three-month minimum sentence. It is the new law."

"What?"

"Of course, you could plead addict which would mean you require drugs for your addiction. Then you would be released in six months to two years." Monterrubio stood and motioned for the guard. "I must go now. There is much to do."

As he hurried off, I noticed Sean's frustration. I could tell his morale was down.

He threw up his hands. "What now."

"Right now, I see no other options. If what he says is true, we don't have much time to get the money for the payoff. Check it out. Jose has someone who can tell us if this formal imprisonment story is true. The US Consulate can too."

"I don't trust that weasel," Sean said.

"This time we take control. We won't turn over the money until he performs."

I sat staring into space and Sean came over and gave me a pat on the back.

"I'll get on it." He started to leave.

"Sean…wait a minute…. You've already done more than I ever expected. I didn't know the Feds would be interested in you too. Nothing more we can do without money. Check things out and go home. Let Bill know everything. I'll wait for him."

Sean left, exasperated, but looking more relaxed than I had seen him since the first day he arrived.

The next visiting day I was happily surprised to see Jose arrive in the afternoon. He brought me a care package from his wife Rosa that contained personal items I could definitely use. More importantly it contained shrimp from the *Estero* around Mazatlán. The fried shrimp were still warm and accompanied with Rosa's homemade salsa. I devoured them.

"Tell Rosa, gracias. This made my day. The best I've had since the last time she made them."

"That will make her happy," he said.

Jose told me that Sean had met with him and asked for a clarification on the possible payoff to the D.A. to prevent my formal imprisonment.

"Sometimes it works, sometimes it don't. It all depends. Bigger fish, more money."

"I hope I'm a small fry."

Jose gave me an update on Felix and Estela. Felix was lying low, hoping the *Federales* would forget about him or find more important things to do. Estela was teaching the children and keeping busy with school. From the look in her eyes, he told me, it was obvious that she felt something special for me. He helped me understand why she could not come to see me in person and delivered the first letter of many she would be writing.

"Sean said Bill is coming soon. Do you want me to help him with anything?

"Fill him in on whatever you find out about my case through your contacts."

"Sure, no problem. Do you think he'll want me to take him to his favorite taco stand with the special guacamole? he asked smiling.

I remembered how Bill unknowingly putting extra spicy guacamole on his tacos and after taking a bite, ran around in circles like a madman, screaming for water.

"*Sin verguenza!*" I laughed. "You wouldn't, would you?

Before Jose left, I made it clear how much I appreciated his help. I asked him to let Felix and Estela know I was doing fine, and hoped to see them soon.

Late that night I began to read the letter from Estela. I could almost hear her voice through the written words. "I was so worried and couldn't find out what happened to you. Everywhere we asked, nobody knew anything. I was so afraid I would never see you again until Felix told me you were alive and well." She mentioned that Felix had contacted his uncle who was an officer in the Navy to try to find out what was going on and how I could be released. "Be safe and remember that last time we kissed," she ended. If she only knew, I thought of that kiss each night as I closed my eyes.

I was called down to the interview room for my first meeting with my government representative, Vice Consul, Parker. He was cordial and more intent on making a good impression than offering to help with my case. I told him about being picked up without cause before I was beaten and tortured. I recounted being taken to a military camp and the sweat tank before arriving at the main prison. He reacted rather passively, telling me that because we were in a foreign country, there was little he could do other than help me contact family and friends. He showed me a list of recommended attorneys. Monterrubio was on the top of the list.

"Why is Monterrubio on the list," I asked.

"We have received no complaints against any of these attorneys."

"Well you have one now. Why was he the only person I was allowed to speak with after being held incommunicado for a week? He made promises, took my family's money and basically did nothing. Now he's come up with a new story and is asking for more money."

"I am unfamiliar with your case and only just recently found out you had been arrested. I will try to look into it, but the Mexicans are often secretive and don't inform us of what they are doing."

This was going nowhere. I suspected Parker knew more than he was letting on. After all, there was the American agent I had seen, who was working with the Mexican Federales. I wouldn't be surprised if he had an office in the consulate.

Obviously, I wasn't looking very happy when I returned to the yard and Q took notice. His first name was Robert like mine, but we called him Q for the first letter of his last name.

"What's up Rob, bad news? asked Q.

"Just tired of the bullshit brother--straight from my own government."

'Right on, I'm with you on that one. They're the ones paying Mexico to put us here for a little stash, while the big boys pay off and go free."

Q had come to Mazatlán to surf and smoke pot with two of his buddies from Long Beach, California. He had met another American on the beach who offered to go in with him on some marijuana. This long-haired surfer turned out to be working with the Mexican Federales. Shortly after the marijuana arrived in the hotel room, the Feds appeared and arrested Q and his two friends. Literally a prisoner in his room for the next two days, his parents were pressured with threatening phone calls. The money didn't come soon enough. He took the rap for everyone and was brought to CPM, while his friends were set free.

Q had been victimized from the start by a small band of Mexican prisoners who habitually broke into his *carraca*, helping themselves to his clothes and food. The turnabout came one evening when he surprised a beefy Mexican about to take off with his clothing and blankets. Catching the thief red-handed infuriated him. In a rage, he pounced on the intruder and smashed his jaw and broke his nose. From then on word was out that Q was no longer easy prey, and anyone would pay a price for invading his space.

With the extreme summer heat and humidity, tempers were short and a small incident could quickly turn into a large free-for-all. Enrique had a friend named Chuy who had made an altar for the prisoners. Images of Jesus Christ and La Virgen de Guadalupe were represented along with other Mexican saints. This was meant to be a sacred refuge for anyone entering. An inmate named Paco was kneeling on a prayer mat when Mudo's two thugs, Nacho and Gorilla, arrived and roughly attempted to drag him away. When he resisted, Gorilla came down with the club and split his head open. Chuy, followed by Tambor and others rushed in to help as Gorilla knocked over the statue of the Virgen de Guadalupe and all hell broke loose. When it was over, Gorilla was sporting a bloody lip and others were tending their wounds as Paco was dragged to Mudo's *carraca*.

It was getting extremely dangerous for those of us who didn't have carracas and lived out in the open amid this chaos. It was Cosey who came up with the idea.

"Why don't we get those boxing gloves Barry's dad sent him and put them to use. Maybe they can let their rage out in the ring instead of busting up each other."

It didn't take long to get more people on the bandwagon and Barry was happy to finally pull the gloves out. We hoped this would let the pressure out before someone got killed.

We set up different weight classifications and everyone chipped in for a purse given to the winner in each division. We would match the fighters as close as we could by weight. Some of the Mexicans were talented and fast, but sitting on top of the heap in the heavyweight division was our own Sully. He was stronger and faster than anyone near his size and had a reach advantage on all of his opponents. No one could touch him and he was hungry for the purse that would cover his next fix.

There was one Mexican boxer that provided more excitement

than anyone else. It was Enrique's friend, Chuy, from the altar. Always mellow with a friendly smile, he was a different person in the ring. When he connected with one of his powerful left hooks, his opponent was either down or seeing stars. Either way the fight was over. Chuy easily won the lightweight division, as Sully became the heavyweight champion.

I was becoming more accustomed to my surroundings and the dysfunctional group in *Correcionales*. I figured out who the junkies were, watching them line up to pick up their fix every morning after *lista*. Gorilla and Nacho were parked in front of Mudo's *carraca*, collecting money and handing out product.

I had often noticed two Americans, Pat and Gene, waiting in line to cop a buy before quickly vanishing into their own *carraca*. Today. I was finally able to talk to them and hear their story. They had been arrested nearly two years earlier making grass oil in a small laboratory on the outskirts of town. Neither one of them had ever used heroin prior to coming to CPM. Now they used it daily to escape the depressing reality of their surroundings.

"Give it a try. It's your ticket to peace." Pat said.

"Not me," I shook my head in the negative. They had given up, and that wasn't in my constitution.

Later in the evening, I settled back on my cot to enjoy the soft sound of Enrique's guitar, camouflage for the shuffling of feet and the ever-present threat of the unknown. The air was warm, and tufts of clouds passed slowly across the moon. Nature was creating her magic, putting on a show that everyone could afford. I was just beginning to relax when Cosey spoke.

"What are we doing here?" he paused, "What are we really doing here?"

"Wasting life's good time," I answered.

Cosey paused, struggling with his thoughts.

"You and I are here on bum raps. Enrique too—and God only knows how many more. But we're here. Why, did you ever ask yourself?"

Of, course, I know the question well," I said.

"What's the answer? That we we're in the wrong place at the wrong time?" he pressed.

"Not only that, but our own government put a bounty on us. More arrests by the Feds means more money from the US."

"I've got this theory that we're meant to be here for a reason. Nothing is chance. We're supposed to be where we are, when we are. Every part of our life is programmed."

"That's one way to look at it, but I need to believe my choices mean something and my actions make a difference."

Cosey rolled over on his back again. "Maybe our choices are predetermined too and you just don't know it. I have to know that I'm programmed to get out of here. That it's in my plan to be moving on and there's something better ahead. It's been seven months now and I don't see anything changing."

"One thing I know for sure" I told him, "Everything changes. You will definitely get out of here, and so will I. Let's hope its feet first and with all our senses. Think positive my friend…we have to be strong and smart to handle whatever is coming."

I closed my eyes and began to think about how absurd our archaic marijuana laws were. "Reefer Madness." The movie was a joke. Incomprehensible, that someone could get busted and have a criminal record for smoking grass. Harming themselves? What about drinking beer or tequila? Our parents enjoyed booze, often to the extreme. I enjoyed an occasional shot of tequila or a couple of beers myself. But what was wrong with lighting up a joint and listening to some music with friends. Laughing together and the getting the munchies were part of the experience. Hell, I knew attorneys and engineers who preferred to light up a joint to relax after work, over drinking booze. I could see potential abuse, but in the same light as alcohol. My generation was looking for something to believe in. Tired of the lies of politicians, who were sacrificing our brothers to wars in far-away lands, dying for people who didn't want to fight for themselves. Then throwing them in jail back home, for smoking a joint. Now, Mexico had changed their laws because of American pressure and money, and we were snared in the trap. What's wrong with this picture I wondered, before drifting off to sleep.

The next day started out with the normal routine. I could hear the leesta, leesta, leesta in my mind before they even started banging on the *carracas*. A few hours later, I was summoned to the visiting area. I had a feeling it was my cousin Bill.

Out of my entire family Bill was the closest to me in age. We shared everything and when we disagreed, we talked it out. We had common interests in books and in sports. He had been on a championship debate team in high school, played basketball, and was elected class president. I made an adventurous journey from California through the South with my college roommate and his brother in the summer '68. We separated after the Memphis Blues Festival when I left to surprise Cousin Bill, who was in the Army and stationed at Ft Bragg. I remembered laughing about it back home years later, as he lit up a joint, and we listened to Sonny Boy Williamson and the Yardbirds. A recent graduate of Sonoma State, he was now a Grateful Dead fan.

Out of our large extended family, Bill was Mom's favorite nephew. He was also a walking encyclopedia, often combining his humor with historical facts. Entering the visitor's room, I saw him sitting at the table with his bushy beard and hair--that was just a little longer than normal.

"Sweet William, or what is it now?" I joked about his nicknames.

"Just call me "Simply Wonderful," he smiled, as we embraced.

"Man, are you a sight for sore eyes"

"I wish I could say the same for you. I was hoping to get an invite to the Instituto Allende and see you there. This place doesn't seem to have the cultural history I was expecting. I even brushed up on my archaeology and the Mayans."

"Do you have a story for me?"

"Just a brief one."

"I'm ready."

"In the height of the classic period, our European ancestors were stuck in the Dark Ages. The Mayans were leap years ahead in astronomy and mathematics."

"I remember reading something about that, but what about the heart and soul of the country?"

"How about Mayan basketball?"

"Basketball?"

"Well, almost basketball, only the hoops were sideways and they dribbled with their elbows. The losing team captain had his heart cut out and eaten raw. Gives a whole new meaning to playing your heart out."

I laughed, "Missed you cousin."

"Sorry it took so long, but there's been a lot going on with try-ing to raise money and hearing so many excuses. In the middle of it all, Barbara called and said she knew what was going on."

"Mom knows?" I asked.

"She had this feeling that something happened to you, so she went to a psychic who mentioned her son, bad associations and trouble. She was driving me and Dinah crazy with her phone calls. After Sean came back without you, we had to tell her."

"Damn it, cousin. This isn't going to be good for her. I've got to get out of here."

"It's better to have her with us than having to lie and BS her. We need to get you out and it's Barbara and Dinah who are really helping with the money. Everyone else was all talk, no action."

"Dinah's helping too?" My sister just barely had enough to keep her beauty shop running. She had her own family to take care of.

"She's helping calm down your Mom and collecting money for you."

"Wow…OK, I'll pay everyone back when I get out. Did Jose give you the rundown?"

"He filled me in on the ride over here. He has a relative in the

Federal offices looking up your case. He doesn't think much of your attorney."

"I don't either. To close to the Feds, and so far he hasn't come through. He wants more money so he can pay off the D.A. Go ahead and meet with him and come see me before you do anything."

"You got it, cuz."

"One more thing. Stop by the restaurant and let Felix know you're here. His uncle is an officer in the Navy and he's trying to get him to help. Let him know I'm OK and have him pass it on to Estela."

"Estela? The teacher you met when I was down here?"

"That's the one."

"Nice lady. Can't figure what she's doing with the likes of you."

"Neither do I, but at least I know she has good taste."

"Maybe you can recite one of these poems in Spanish, from the man," he said handing me an Octavio Paz poetry book. And here's a letter from your Mom."

Bill hesitated, took a deep breath and gave me a hug.

"Hang in there. I'll take care of things and be back before you know it."

I felt some relief knowing that Bill would stop at nothing to help me. I now had family going to bat for me, and it gave me hope.

The next day Cosey asked if I would like to join the CPM Bridge group.

"You play Bridge here?

Cosey nodded. "We need a player. Terry's been sick for almost a week and were one short."

"Count me in. Been a while, but I'm up for the challenge."

I learned about two other Americans at the game. Don, in his forties, had been arrested at a roadblock with his wife, Shirley. The soldiers found an unregistered hunting rifle in their camper and arrested both of them, confiscating their boat, camper, and hunting dogs. They were owners of a yacht marina in Lake Tahoe. Don was bitter as he recounted the story of his arrest and beating. His attorney had already received over seventy thousand pesos for promises that had not been kept. His wife Shirley was incarcerated in the women's section, *Mujeres*. She was only allowed to see him on visiting days.

Yoshi was an inscrutable bridge player with a sly sense of humor. He was quiet and kept to himself, but I couldn't help but notice an inner strength and confidence. I had noticed him going through a karate routine or meditating at different times of the day. One day he opened up and told me a little about himself. He had been born in an internment camp in Arizona where his mother had been taken with her family from their farm in Washington. She was an American citizen of Japanese ancestry and we were at war with Japan. Later, moving to California, his father had designed an acclaimed Bonsai garden and Aka had learned from the master. He had also guided his son in meditation. Yoshi confided to me that he was still seeing into nothingness, and looking for enlightenment.

I received my first refresher course in Bridge by actually playing. The total concentration required to be competitive was definitely good exercise for my brain. Don was the real bridge expert in our group, teaching us with his play while giving us a little historical perspective. He informed us that George Washington, Dwight D Eisenhower, and Winston Churchill all loved the game, and had been avid bridge players.

That night, I sat down to read Mom's letter. She lost all of her objectivity, revealing a depth of uncontrolled emotion I had never seen.

"What do you think you're doing, getting in trouble and not telling me? Don't ever think that when you are in a situation like this, I don't feel it. I brought you into this world and we are always connected. I knew something had happened and was going crazy trying to find out what was going on. "Whatever you need to survive until you are safely home, I will take care of it." She told me to be strong and that she would soon be sending a care package to me. At the end, she sent her love and apologized for being so hard on me in the beginning of the letter.

I closed my eyes and could see her loving smile while feeling her pain. This was exactly why I had wanted to keep this from her. I would do anything to keep from hurting her. This would be over soon, I promised myself.

Two days later I was summoned to the visiting quarters. I was excited. Bill had not wasted any time. As I entered the room with Bill and Monterrubio, I could tell from the look on their faces this would not be a good meeting.

"You have been formally imprisoned," my attorney said rather matter-of-factly. "I can file an *amparo* in Hermosillo and you can be set free. If I don't, you are facing a five-year, three-month sentence."

I was in shock. "Your story keeps changing. You keep promising and not coming through. Why should I believe you now?" I asked him. Bill was watching intently.

"Things don't always go as planned in my country, but I have been in this situation before and I know how to get you out. This is like a "habeas corpus" and will state that the judge was faulty in his decision to imprison you because there is lack of sufficient evidence. It is your only chance."

He told us it would be necessary to "grease a few palms" to speed things up. The cost, only twenty-five thousand pesos, the same as we were going to spend with the Judge.

"We'll get back to you. I want to speak to my cousin---alone."

After he left, I threw my hands up in the air.

"For Chrissakes, what kind of a merry-go-round are we riding on? This is impossible!"

"Beats me, cuz. I don't believe anything the guy says."

"Let me think about this", holding my hands to my head. "We need to check on the *amparo* and filing in Hermosillo, and what the chances are it can work. Just like before, he gets no money until I'm free. You haven't given him anything yet, have you?"

"Not one cent."

"Good, talk to Jose. Find out if this is for real. If not, we'll figure out another plan. No way I'm going to spend five years here."

Billy felt my anger.

"Don't worry cousin. One way or another you'll be leaving this hellhole."

The next day was unsettling for me. I would have sworn Mudo had posted a sign alerting everyone about my formal imprisonment. I had told no one except for Cosey and my poker buddies, Randy, Gary, Long John, and Rich. Over the next few days, a steady stream of hustlers pecked at me from sunrise to sunset trying to get me to take something to relax and help me sleep. Chico was pushing the *chiva* and offering a free taste. I was in no mood to numb myself with anything. My mind had to be clear. I had no faith in Monterrubio and had to figure out a backup plan. I started playing chess to stay active and exercise my mind. I enjoyed strategizing, making moves and counter moves, while envisioning far ahead the variables that could come up. A good escape plan could require all of that and I wanted to be sharp. I held my own with all my chess opponents, until I came up against Sully.

Sully was the slickest con man and rip off artist at CPM. I had been warned to be wary of him from others who had personal items snatched by him. I already knew that he was an addict and would do just about anything to get a fix. In spite of everything, he was a fascinating person who happened to be from my hometown. I soon found out more about his life and experiences as he let down his guard and opened up to me. He talked about how he made money as a chess hustler in LA, letting his opponent gain confidence by losing some early games before raising the stakes. After the bet went up, Sully would clean his clock. As I spent more time with him, he began to teach me some of his hustles and card tricks. I wondered what he might have become if he had used that intelligence in the straight world.

I decided to try one his hustles as a challenge to myself. Could I really do it and keep my cool? I practiced the short change scam with Sully until I had it down. It was time to test out the new student. I'd better get it right, since I wasn't sure what would happen to me if I were caught. At the store I purchased a couple of sodas and various snacks. After exchanging the pesos as I had been taught by Sully, I left with more money than I had started with. I was elated. It worked. My self-confidence was up, but no way I wanted to do it again. It may have been second nature to him, but for me, I had passed a test and that was enough. I would figure a way to return the money without anyone knowing.

Tonight, Sully was singing a soulful "People Get Ready" as Enrique strummed softly. A rain began to fall and the compound was turned in to a pool of water. I could see that a really bad rain could create havoc as I remembered the hurricane that had come while I was visiting last October. Jose's taxi couldn't make it to my hotel and I had waded back in water up to my waste. Windows were broken, roofs were damaged, homes were flooded, and from my hotel I could see boats capsize on the ocean. The next day when the sun came out, all was back to normal at the beach resorts. What the tourists didn't see, was the cleanup from the destruction of homes and roads in outlying areas.

Thursday was visitor's day and Jose came to see me again, bringing news, and more of Rosa's delicious home cooked food.

He smiled at me. "First let me get this out of the way," handing me a bag. "From Rosa."

This time it was tamales, rice and beans. I wasn't sure if I could wait until lunchtime. It smelled so good.

Jose went straight to the point. "You won't believe what I found out."

"Tell me."

"You know Rosa's *prima* works in the Federal offices. It took us a little time to convince her and she had to be careful, but she found out what's really going on. In your file there's not much about you at all, mostly questions."

"Really?"

"They don't have anything other than you are an associate of a man they are interested in named Ron Warren. It seems he has been here a number of times and is suspected of flying out planeloads of grass. He seems to be connected with someone in government, but she didn't find a name. Your file mentions one *cigaro* found in a portfolio with his name on it. You've been framed, my friend."

That all made sense and was close to what I had figured out myself. I fell into a net that had been put out for Ron and then they found out they had the wrong man. Didn't matter to them, more Americans arrested, meant more money from my government. They get paid, guilty or innocent. The main question in my mind. Did Ron know he was under suspicion and give me the Safari to set me up? Someday, I would find out the truth.

"Bill came by and told me what's going on with your attorney and the *amparo*," Jose continued. "I checked with my contact. Filing the *amparo* is for real, but works less than half the time. Bill's going with Felix, to talk with his uncle."

"Shit, I'm frustrated Jose. My attorney's a shyster. Every junkie is trying to get money or pushing me to take *chiva*. I feel like I'm ready to explode."

Jose stared at me, serious, and began his sentence slowly.

"I hope you won't be upset at me my friend, but I think I have just the remedy to lighten your load."

"What's that?"

"Do you remember the *señorita* who worked at Los Jardines and took care of you when you were in bad shape with that infection?"

"You mean Nanci?"

He nodded, "She found out you're here and wants to come visit and help you again."

THE GREAT WHEELCHAIR ESCAPE

"You mean she would actually come here to see me?"

"She's planning on it. She had a vision that you need her. She'll be here this afternoon. I thought you might want a little notice and get cleaned up."

A big grin spread across my face.

"Jose, I can't stand it. First you bring me food from the best cook in Mazatlán, then you tell me a beautiful *señorita* is coming to visit me. You must come more often."

"What are friends for?"

"Give Rosa a big thank you...and you're right, I'd better get cleaned up."

Jose left with the morning visitors and I ate Rosa's tamales, savoring every bite.

Now I would clean up and find something decent to wear.

I met Nanci on my second trip to Mazatlán. I had booked a room at Los Jardines, which included a health food restaurant and juice bar, in a beautiful tropical setting. My mornings would begin with a fresh squeezed juice by Nanci before going out to surf the waters of the Pacific. She was nineteen years old with dark eyes, brown skin, and a smile that was irresistible. By the third day we had made a connection and decided we should go out together. She wanted to show me her town.

We dined at a popular seafood restaurant with an open air palapa, right on the beach. Seated next to the sand, we watched the sunset over the ocean as strolling musicians serenaded us. Smiling, we left hand in hand, to visit Nanci's favorite dancing spot which was also out in the open and under a palapa. The stars twinkled from above and we joyously moved to the music for hours. It was a night I would never forget.

The next morning, vomiting and with fever, I had no desire to move. Nanci had not seen me leave the room and was worried. She stopped by to see me after work. One look and she immediately went into action. She cleaned me up and put on fresh clothes before heading home to get herbal teas and family remedies to cure me. For the next few days she stopped by to check on me daily and slowly nursed me back to health. This was when I learned about her boyfriend, Ricardo, who was a musician and traveled half the year, with a girl in every city. I could tell she was smitten by him, and any ideas I may have had, I buried deep inside. On the morning of my departure she came by to say goodbye and I held her in a long embrace. Both of us felt the connection and as we separated, our eyes told no secrets. Neither of us would forget. I often wondered if I should have been more insistent. Now I was in trouble again, and she was coming to me.

I needed to find some water and clean clothes.

"Sully, I need your help brother."

"What's up, Rob?"

I explained my situation and that I would like some privacy with my visitor. I'd seen him make deals before with *carraca* owners for couples on visiting day.

"No problem, I'll make the deal. You work on getting cleaned up."

I was tense and nervous. I'd been trying to survive my ordeal for so long; my body was tight. I needed to relax. I took some deep breaths and closed my eyes. When I opened them again, I saw her and almost pinched myself to make sure I wasn't dreaming. She looked even more radiant than I remembered. I took her hand. Since it was visiting day, the yard was full of people lost in their own world. Most didn't take notice of us. Where was Sully? Just as I was about to give up, he appeared, introduced himself and invited us to follow him. On the way, I passed the smiling face of Cosey, and caught a wink from Q.

Inside the *carraca* was a bed that looked clean and freshly made. A pleasing tropical fragrance permeated the room. What a pleasant surprise. Now I knew why Sully had taken so long.

I held her hand as we sat together.

"How did you find me?" I asked.

"Oh, a little bird told me. You'd be surprised what I know about you, Roberto. Sometimes I close my eyes and remember the last time I saw you. If it wasn't for Ricardo…shh, I touched her lips with my finger.

"It doesn't matter, I said. What matters is that you're here, and now I know you felt the same as I did last…she put her finger to my lips.

We embraced and were both shaking, trembling. I could feel a heat leaving her body and her fire engulfed me. There were no thoughts, just… passion. The first time I felt a great explosion and then relaxation, as if I were floating on soft white clouds. Connected, we started again and slowly took a journey to places we had never gone before…together.

Suddenly there was a knock on the door. It was Sully's voice. "Time's up!"

Must have lost track of time completely. I left the clouds and came back down to reality. Way too soon, I thought.

Holding her hand, I walked Nanci to the exit. Our eyes connected, then she gave me a quick kiss and was gone. I was stunned to be back in the real world and felt an emptiness inside. Was that a dream? But that night I slept better than I could remember for a long, long time.

# 7

## *The Tunnel*

**W**ord must have gotten out around the compound about my lovely visitor. The next morning there were smiles, winks, and thumbs up from the guys—probably wondering how I was able to get such a lovely young lady to visit me. Randy guided me into his *carraca* where Rich, John, and Barry were already waiting for me. From their serious looks I knew something was up. I had been invited to a secret gathering. Our voices were drowned out by a Bob Dylan song--"The Times They Are A Changin."

Rich wiped his glasses. "Words out about your formal imprisonment and I want you to know we're sorry to hear your deal didn't come through. We voted, and it was unanimous."

"Right on," said Randy.

"Be ready to take the bull by the horns," said Long John.

"Damn straight," Barry chirped in.

"Before I tell you the plan, I want your word that whatever you decide, nothing leaves this room," Rich continued.

"Loose lips sink ships. You've got my word," I promised.

We talked for almost an hour. The plan was to dig a tunnel under Rich's *carraca*, which was next to the twenty-five-foot high wall. Four feet down and less than twelve feet across, we would come out just beyond the high wall. The shorter second wall, about six feet high, topped with barbed wire, was less than thirty feet away. Wire cutters had already been smuggled in. They had been digging for over three weeks, making progress slowly, but safely. Disposing of the dirt had been the main challenge and it looked like they had found a solution. A fake wall was created between Rich's *carraca* and that of his neighbors, Barry and John. At eighteen inches wide with a ten-foot height, the space would easily hold the dirt that had been stored in laundry bags under the cots. An optical illusion had been created with posters, photos, and shelves full of miscellaneous items that covered the fake wall and camouflaged the hidden compartment. Mick, who Rich had taken under his wing, was now his *carraca* mate. He was short and agile enough to handle the bulk of the digging. He was still getting his daily fix and Rich had been unsuccessful so far in weaning him off heroin.

I learned about previous tunnel escape attempts at CPM. One had taken place about three years ago and even though faced with a slew of problems including a broken water line, five prisoners had managed to escape. Most recently, a group of political prisoners in *Considerados* had been trapped inside their tunnel by the guards during their attempt. They had been captured and immediately transferred to *Separos* with the loss of all privileges and possessions.

Our plan was to break out during *El Dia de Los Presos*, the "Prisoner's Day" celebration that was to take place in less than three weeks. Food, drink, and wandering musicians contributed to the biggest weekend of the year at CPM. Families, friends, and lovers joined the fiesta which lasted late into the night. Girlfriends and wives would be allowed to sleep over and there would be plenty of liquor for guards and prisoners alike. Live music from wandering *bandas* would continue through the wee hours of the morning. By the time anyone would notice us missing, we would be long gone.

I was asked about providing transportation since I had friends and contacts in the area.

"Can you have someone pick us up, once we get outside?' Rich asked.

"I should be able to arrange that and maybe more. I'll start putting the pieces in place and get back to you."

"We also need you to be our yard guard. You're the only one of us living outside who can keep an eye out for trouble."

"Yard guard, I like it. Finally got myself a title."

Late afternoon, I had a visitor. It was Bill. Now I would get the skinny on the *Amparo*.

"Can't get enough of this place, eh cousin?

"Like a magnet," he joked. "By the way, Felix and Estela hooked me up with a sweet one."

"Oh no, Sweet William with a 'sweet one'. What's the world coming to?"

"I'm liking it here. Can stay as long as you want."

"Good to know, but I may have something for you back home. Give me some good news."

Billy fidgeted with his glasses and took a deep breath.

"OK, I'll start with Monterubbio and the *Amparo*. I checked with Jose, and even met with Felix's uncle. They all say an *Amparo* can work, but not without money and connections. Over half of them fail. And it has to be filed in the District Court in Hermosillo."

"How much time does it take?"

"We should have an answer within thirty days. I would give Monterubbio expense money only. The rest goes in the bank until you walk out, a free man."

"Good work, let's give it a try. As long as we don't risk our money upfront, not much to lose. I'll be working on another option. You can head back tomorrow."

'No problem. That gives me one more night to spend with Lupe."

"Lupe? Is that who they set you up with?"

"The one and only."

"Sounds like she made an impression. Enjoy your last night. You deserve it. When you get back home, find Triumph Dave."

"Where do I find him?"

"Last I heard he was living in Manhattan Beach with Didi's sister, Brenda. Let him know his services may be needed down here and make sure his pilot's license is current. You'll get a call from Jose."

"Got it...Oops, almost forgot," he handed me a letter, "Felix says this is from Estela."

"Thanks for remembering, cousin. Anything else?"

"Just one more thing... Did you know marijuana was brought to Mexico as hemp by the Europeans and Cortez in the 1500's. It was planted and used for rope, clothing, and even pain relief."

"No, I didn't know that"

"Here's what's really interesting. True story...Years later, Pancho Villa's men were smoking it. Called it *grifo*. Our troops tried like hell, but couldn't catch Pancho. Started rollin their own *grifo*. They liked it so much they left Pancho in Mexico, and brought home the *grifo*."

I smiled, "I'm gonna miss you cousin." A hug and he was gone.

Back at my cot, I read the letter from Estela:

She wrote about how the children she was teaching helped fill the emptiness inside she felt from missing me... "I brought flowers to the Virgen de Guadalupe today and prayed for your safety and freedom. You are always in my thoughts and my heart." I put the letter to my nose and could smell her perfume.

I opened up the Octavio Paz poetry book, "Los Novios" that Bill had brought and read—"*Comen naranjas, cambien besos como las olas cambien sus espumas.*"

Poetically, it described our last magical kiss.

Soon it was visiting day again. Engrossed in a book by the name of "Papillon", I was oblivious to the family reunions going on around me. I admired the mental toughness and the determination of the main character whose experience had similarities to my own. Out of the corner of my eye, I saw a figure that looked strangely familiar. I almost fell off my cot. I caught a glimpse of his blondish- brown hair and the back of his head as he followed Gary into the *carraca*. Improbable, but it sure looked like him. I had to get a closer look.

Jon Lemna was a good friend of mine from the San Diego area. We knew each other well and had many unforgettable dinners together while going to sports events and music concerts. He had a ten-acre ranch home in Ramona and owned the Red Dog Trading Company. Jon bought and sold Navajo art, white and aqua turquoise, and silver jewelry from Mexico. I had set up distribution for his unique white turquoise in Northern and Southern California. Last time I had seen him, he had showed me an ancient Mastadon tusk that had been found somewhere near his ranch. Jon had a wonderful sense of humor and was one of my favorite people. I walked over to the *carraca* and leaned in.

Jon was sitting down scribbling notes while Gary was talking.

"I hear someone has a Mastadon tusk for sale," I interrupted.

Gary stopped talking and they both looked at me, mouths open. Jon was temporarily speechless and his eyes opened wide as a smile spread across his face.

"Robert," he exclaimed. "What the hell are you doing here?"

"Man, are you a sight for sore eyes," I responded.

"You two know each other," said Gary, surprised.

"Old and good friends. Let me finish up with Gary here and we'll talk."

"Sure, I'm right outside. Gary can direct you."

'No, I'll come get you. You two can use my *carraca*." Gary said.

A few minutes later I was alone with Jon. He told me he had known Gary for years. They had met as students at the University of Illinois. Word had gotten out through the grapevine that Gary needed help and John had the contacts in Mexico that could get him out. He told me about one man who was the "fixer" and connected all the way up to the Federal government in Mexico City.

"Most of the time the local attorneys just take money and do nothing." he told me.

His man Mel was solid and would not take a case he could not fix. He told me Gary was coming out soon and he would talk to Mel about helping me. I let him know that Bill and Mom were doing everything they could to get me out and we had an attorney who was questionable, if not completely useless. I gave him Bill's contact number and he left with a hug and words of encouragement.

That day Gary and I had our first good talk. We soon realized that we had mutual acquaintances and knew people in the same social circle. He had been living in the LA area, owned his own music publishing company, and was connected to some up and coming rock groups. Although aware of the tunnel plan, he didn't want any part of it, feeling certain that Jon would get him out.

I took my title of "Yard guard" seriously. I would stroll within eyesight of Rich's *carraca* all hours of the day or night. Any unusual occurrences in the courtyard would be reported by me immediately. Almost two weeks had passed and nothing much had been out of the ordinary. Today was different. I was up early and took my morning stroll. The door was open a crack and just inside the *carraca*, I noticed a small pile of dirt that hadn't been there before. When I was sure no one was looking, I entered the *carraca*. The trail of dirt began under Mick's cot. I woke up Rich and we quickly cleaned up the pile. Mick was dead to the world.

After *lista*, we met in Randy's *carraca*.

"The bag under the cot had a hole in it and somehow the dirt was dragged out," Rich said.

I had thought long and hard about it. "Rats." I guessed.

"What?"

"A huge one visited me when I slept on the cement. They seem to be active in the wee hours of the morning."

"I'll be ready tonight," said Rich.

"Didn't Mick notice anything?"

"Mick's been digging for hours every night. He's exhausted."

'Is he cleaning up his act, or do you have to take care of his habit to keep him going?" I asked.

"I'm worried. Seems like the pressure is getting to him and he's taking more *chiva* now than before. I'm doing everything I can. Pray for us."

I told Rich that I knew firsthand how junkies could lose all sense of value if they were strung out and needed a fix. They would scam good friends and even family. Mick was my main worry in all of this. I gave Rich the good news about Triumph Dave and a plane ride home, but told him not to mention my part in this to anyone, especially Mick. If he started going through withdrawals and needed a fix, he could do or say anything….and bring us all down. *El Dia de Los Presos* was coming up soon and Rich guaranteed the tunnel would be finished ahead of schedule.

That night as I went for my evening stroll, I came to the altar that Chuy had put together. I stopped to take it all in. The candles were lit and the portraits of the "Virgen de Guadalupe" and "Jesus" were illuminated. Yoshi was sitting in lotus position, meditating. I remembered Rich asking me to "pray for us". Estela had told me in her letter that she had brought flowers to the "*Virgen*" and prayed.

"Sit down, Don Roberto," Chuy invited, "Everyone is welcome here."

"Thank you."

I sat down and bowed my head in prayer, closed my eyes and relaxed. Time disappeared. I could feel something powerful, spiritual, consuming my entire body. I let my mind go, free of thoughts, and felt something I couldn't describe in words. It was like I could feel the spirit of God within. I don't know how much time passed, but afterwards I felt cleansed, like something heavy had been lifted off of me. Although I'm a spiritual being, I don't belong to any one religious order, but take something from all of them. Having gone through the rituals of Protestant and Baptist churches as a boy and the meditation of Buddhism and Yoga in college, I believed there were different paths that all lead to the same place. Finally, I rose and Chuy walked beside me to visit Enrique. He was softly playing his guitar and smiled when he saw the two of us.

I was getting into a routine and nothing much was changing. After morning *lista*, I would have breakfast with Cosey then walk around and greet a few friends before heading over to our Bridge game. I had improved my skills in Bridge, learning about when to play my Trump card and take the tricks. Don was still the master, but I was becoming a respected challenger. In the afternoons I did some reading and wrote letters while listening to Enrique and his guitar. I continued being a regular at the nightly poker games, enjoying the camaraderie and getting regular updates on the tunnel.

Then Mudo and the warden hit us with their latest plan to extort money. This time it was the mail. Our letters from home had not been delivered in over a week. We depended on our mail to keep connected with family and friends and to keep our sanity. Money needed for our basic necessities, like food and medicine often arrived as money orders. Not getting our mail was a very big deal. Chico told us that Mudo could help us get the mail flowing again for five thousand pesos each.

No doubt this scam was thought up by Mudo and the warden. We decided to go another route. We gave Gretchen the phone numbers of our families so she could let them know what was happening. We told her to have them put pressure on their legislators and representatives. She would also go to the American consulate with a petition signed by all of us demanding they become involved to restore delivery of our mail.

On the next visiting day, Gretchen arrived with a carton of vanilla ice cream and a bag of fresh fruit for both of us.

"The consul's office has the petition," she said, spooning out the softening ice cream into plastic saucers. "I gave it to Parker."

"The man himself," I sighed. "We'll see if he actually does something."

"I called the families and they were really upset, Gretchen said. "Parker should be getting a few calls from Washington too."

"I like the sound of that," said Cosey.

"I second that. Way to go, Gretchen."

"Take a look at this," she said, handing a newspaper to Cosey.

"It's in Spanish. All I recognize is Monterubbio's name." Cosey handed me the paper.

I looked at the headlines "*Denunciaron a Monterrubio—sus Victimas.*"

"What's it say?" Cosey asked.

"It says our shyster attorney was picked up for embezzling clients."

'You mean he might be joining us?"

"It doesn't mention what will happen to him, but with all his contacts, I doubt if we'll be seeing him unless he's broke and can't pay the *mordida*. I'll bet he's extra good at greasing palms when it comes to himself."

That night I received the latest update on the tunnel. They had passed twelve feet under the wall were beginning to come up. Just a few more days... if Mick could keep it together. Rich had tried to make him cut down on his habit, but he was getting belligerent. Everything was ready on my end. Jose had already come by to give me an update. He would be ready to pick us up by car and take us to a private airstrip where Triumph Dave would fly us out. Everything was on for *El Dia de Los Presos* in three more days. I was excited and a little nervous, but at least my life would be in my own hands. I was sick and tired of hearing the false promises of Monterrubio as he pressured my family for more money. I was tense and didn't sleep well that night.

The shrill sound of whistles ripped through the air.

"Leesta, Leesta, Leesta!"

I woke up and watched the theatrics. Something was up. Gorilla, Nacho, and Chico were scampering around the yard pounding on *carracas* as Mudo in his sunglasses was standing next to the warden and armed prison guards. Federal and local police surrounded them. It was way too early for *lista*.

"Leesta, Leesta, Leesta!"

One by one, carraca doors started opening and sleepy half-dressed occupants stumbled into their places in line. We were told get in line and not to move.

Like a dog smelling his bone, the warden entered Rich's carraca to find the prize with the Federales close behind. We could hear noises of furniture being moved and items being busted up. Then everything was quiet, and we were all herded down to a small, sweltering room below. In a few minutes our number was reduced by two, as Rich and Mick were pulled out. That was the last I ever saw of them.

Over an hour passed before we were brought back to *Correcionales*. As *carraca* owners entered their homes, it was apparent that much had been stolen. Enrique, with his missing leg had a ringside seat. I asked him what he had seen and he told me that all the *carracas* had been entered, but only the ones owned by Americans had been relieved of belongings.

I felt numb all over. I had begun to like and admire Rich. The fact that we were working together as a team to be free, gave me hope and inspiration. He and Mick had been at the most risk, and paid the heaviest price for failure. Hopefully, the warden would be satisfied with the two of them and wouldn't try to widen the net to look for co-conspirators. I knew Mick would be going through withdrawals and could easily tell them anything. No way to know for sure how they found out about the tunnel. I had to call Jose to let him know what had happened.

That night during the poker game with Randy, John, and Barry, we discussed the bust and what to expect next. Now that we were all down, we expected Mudo and the warden to lash out and make us all pay for the tunnel, one way or another. As the days passed, we were watched more closely than ever with unannounced searches at all hours of the day. I had a feeling something big was coming. I just didn't know when, or what.

I had just returned from the Bridge game and began to relax on my cot when I found Gorilla at my side. He forcefully let me know that Mudo required my presence… immediately! When I hesitated, he yanked on my arm trying to pull me up. I pulled out of his grasp and he went backwards almost falling down. Fortunately, he didn't have his big club handy and merely gave me a stare down before beckoning me to follow him.

Chico was waiting at the door and let me in. Mudo was stretched out on his bed facing a flip-flopping picture on his TV. He paid little attention to me while telling Chico to pass along some information. His manner was so casual I felt that whatever Chico had to say would be of little interest. But I was wrong. The word had come directly from the warden. My attorney had removed himself from my case.

"What!" I stammered.

"He have a big *fiesta* with *mariachis* and lots of food and drink. Many people at party, even *Federales*. He use your money…everybody happy."

I shook my head.

"You try some *chiva* to relax," Chico offered. "Mudo say free today, you no pay. He feel sorry for you." For the first time I was tempted to take him up on his offer.

Ten minutes later I was in the warden's office being questioned as to why I hadn't come earlier. There were papers regarding my formal imprisonment that my attorney had neglected to complete. The warden's assistant asked me questions as he typed up the report. Since I no longer had an attorney, anything in process would stop immediately.

When I returned to the yard it seemed that everyone knew

about my situation. Native tom toms couldn't have spread the word any faster. A steady stream of hustlers hit on me and there was Chico holding up his *chiva*. I didn't even look his way.

This was too much to handle after the busted tunnel. I felt ready to explode and needed to unwind. I decided that if I was going to take something to relax, it would be with someone I knew. Sully was happy to see me give it a try.

"I heard about what happened Rob. This will mellow you out. It's the only thing that keeps me going in this funky place."

I gave him twenty pesos which bought enough *chiva* for both of us. I was only going to take a little snort, while he was going to shoot up. I followed Sully to a private spot in one of the *carracas* he used for his business. He set up two lines for me on a mirror while I rolled up a crisp ten-peso bill. I hesitated, then snorted a line in each nostril. A slight itch in my nose was soon followed by warm relaxing sensation traveling through my body and my senses. Soon it seemed like I was in the middle of a circus with many different acts going on around me all at once.

Outside I ran into Randy and Cosey and my words seemed to flow smooth and relaxed. I aimlessly strolled around the yard, almost floating. Then, I began to itch on my arms, chest, and neck. A queasiness began building in my stomach and I felt like I was going to vomit. I hurried to get back to the *baño*, but didn't make it. Everything came out right in front of Mudo's carraca. Looking at the splattered mess, I didn't think Chico would be offering me anymore free *chiva*. Just thinking about it, gave me the shivers.

# 8

## Confrontation

It was early afternoon a few days later when my reading was interrupted by a loud whoop coming from Randy and Gary's *carraca*. I moved as fast as I could, not knowing what to expect. Gary had a shit eating grin on his face and was holding up a letter.

"He did it, Rob! I'm going home, thanks to Jon."

Randy, Gary and I slapped high fives. We were so excited it must have looked like we were doing our own version of the Irish Jig. With all the bad news lately, it was uplifting to know that one of us was actually going home. If it happened for one, it could happen for more. The wide smile on Gary's face told the story. I was hoping to be next in line. The wizard "Mel," had secured Gary's release. It had cost over sixteen thousand dollars, but he would soon be a free man.

A few days later when Jon showed up to escort him out, I felt mixed emotions. Happy for Gary, yet wishing I was walking out with them. Jon understood and looked at me with a promising smile.

"I'll be talking to Mel next week about your case. He only takes one case at a time. I'll try to get you first in line. When he's ready, we'll need to put ten thousand dollars in the bank escrow account to get him moving. Hang in there."

Ten thousand dollars? Thank God I hadn't tried to discourage Mom from mortgaging her home. I wondered if she had gone ahead with her plans. Whatever the "fixer" required in trust would be needed quickly, or I'd probably lose him.

Randy invited me to move in with him. He didn't have to twist my arm. I jumped at the chance to leave the yard and get away from the hovering junkies and hustlers, as well as the watchful eyes of Mudo's henchmen. Besides being able to read and write in peace, there was Randy's fabulous music collection that should definitely lift my spirits. To keep my body in shape I would have a private place to do pushups and some yoga stretching; at least the cobra, the dog, and the cat.

I would return my cot to Sully. I knew I could trust him to keep an eye on Enrique. They were already working together to make a few extra bucks when Sully set up serenades for couples on visiting days. I stopped by to tell Cosey the good news and let him know that Sully would be using my cot. We talked for a while about Monterrubio getting busted. Both of us hoped that he would end up just as miserable as us.

"Do you know where Enrique is? I want to let him know where I'm going."

"I thought you knew," Cosey said. "They took him away this morning."

"What? Where?"

"Those sores on his good leg got worse and it was really swollen. He was in a lot of pain. Chuy and Tambor made sure he was taken out for treatment."

"Are they taking care of his guitar too?" I asked, noticing it wasn't in its usual spot.

"As soon as the guards carried him out, Gorilla snatched his guitar. It's with Mudo now."

"Shit!"

I picked up my books, a small bag of belongings, and headed to my new home.

"Desperado" by the Eagles was playing as I entered the *carraca*. How appropriate, I thought.

"You didn't have to put that song on just for me," I told Randy.

"Don't worry, there's plenty more where that came from."

"I hope so," I laughed.

I received a letter from my mother in the day's mail. "There is a lot of talk about President Ford demanding the release of all prisoners in Mexico," she wrote, "to serve the balance of their sentences in the United States. We're praying for quick action." She sent me a news clipping about an organization funded by Hugh Hefner to legalize marijuana called NORML.

I showed the letter to Randy. When he finished reading, he simply shrugged.

"That's not news," he said. "We heard the same story months ago about the prisoners. Legalizing pot sounds good, but it'll never happen."

The next day Randy received a letter from home that put him into a rage. He let out a loud yell and then began hitting and kicking anything in sight. I tried to find out what had happened and calm him down. He mumbled something about his girlfriend and how he had to get out and back home immediately. Then he screamed that his attorney ripped off his family's money. He crumbled up the letter and threw it in the trash and stomped outside. He didn't want to talk about it. Bad news from home could put any of us into angry fit and deep depression. I could understand how some had become addicted to heroin to escape the helplessness and pain they felt inside. I was even more determined to keep fit and have all my options open for escape. Sure, there was a chance that Jon would come through, but I wouldn't count on it. I would figure something else out that would work for both Randy and myself.

I'd been feeling ever since the tunnel bust, that something was up with Mudo. His mail extortion scam hadn't worked because we had gone directly to our families and the American Counsel. Now the mail was arriving on time, unopened. But something was in the air. I could feel it.

We were hit twice on the same day. After morning *lista*, we received a list with the names of prisoners that were going to be transferred out of *Correcionales*. They would lose their *carracas* and most of their belongings. Coincidentally, the only names on the list were Americans that owned *carracas*. Mudo could fix everything for just five hundred pesos each. Anyone who did not pay, would be transferred to the Grande, beginning next week.

Later that afternoon Cosey burst into our *carraca*.

"No more *baño*," he said holding up his key. "Locks been changed. They're scamming us again."

"Try yours." he told us.

Randy and I both went to try our keys. Same result. The lock had been changed. Most of us had paid two hundred-fifty pesos for a key to have access to the "executive" bathroom. It had a relatively clean toilet and a shower that worked some of the time. The thought of having to use the other filthy, fly infested diarrhea den, where a few dead bodies had been found, was enough to rouse our group to rebellion.

"What the fuck?" said Randy, as he pounded on the locked *baño* door.

"Enough," I said, "He's going to keep pulling this crap until we stand up to him. We need to get together and come up with a plan. We have strength in numbers."

"No shit, I'll pass the word. We need to stand together on this," said Cosey. "How bout we all meet after morning *lista* in your *carraca*."

"Do it! Randy said.

That afternoon I heard Chico indoctrinating two new arrivals. I knew the pitch by heart. He had already delivered his welcoming speech, taken the newcomers to Mudo for the shakedown, and was now working on the price policy. The next step would be to offer a little *chiva,* then walk away and let the men flounder for themselves.

Moments later, the two men were alone, standing bewildered in the center of the shuffling circle. I could tell they were Americans. Both were in their early to mid-twenties. One was of medium build with blond hair, and quite nervous. The other had a hard, lean body and brown hair. He was the calmer of the two. They looked lost and lonely, searching for a friendly face.

As I introduced myself, the tension drained from their faces. I invited them into the *carraca* for a cool drink and to meet Randy.

The tanned, blond American was named Jack. He and his girl-friend, Myrna, were from Santa Cruz, California. They had been in Mexico on vacation, traveling the scenic backroads in their van. They had met Greg on a beach in Nayarit. Greg was a Vietnam veteran and the nephew of former astronaut, John Glenn. He was hitching a ride to Oceanside, California where his parents lived. He told me about his attempt to start a peanut farm and the challenges he had faced. At the roadblock outside Mazatlán, the three were detained when soldiers found organic tea packed among Jack and Myrna's food supply. The soldiers thought the tea was marijuana and arrested them. When Jack adamantly denied the charge and showed hostility towards them, he was taken aside and beaten. The van was confiscated and the prisoners brought to CPM. Myrna was locked up in the women's section.

That night Jack and Greg slept on the floor of our *carraca.* In the morning Chico, Gorilla, Pipino and Nacho, appeared at our door to collect five hundred pesos from each of our guests for sleeping in the *carraca.* Randy and I branded the attempt to extort money from the newcomers as outrageous. We advised them flatly not to pay. They didn't need our advice. Jack and Greg stood firm of their own free will —even when Mexico's mini-version of the Dirty Dozen threatened to imprison them with the crazies and murderers in *Separos*.

"Work detail for one week," Chico growled. Then he laughed as they were leaving, at the thought of the Americans cleaning the filthy toilets on their hands and knees.

"I have a feeling Greg won't be with us very long," Randy said.

"Why? Because of his uncle?"

"That and his father. He's a Marine Corps General at Camp Pendleton."

By ten am the next morning we had our group ready to stand up against Mudo. Besides Randy and myself, our group included John and Barry, Cosey, Yoshi, and Q. We all agreed we had to be smart about how we presented our demands to Mudo. He respected strength and ruled by fear. How could we present a win/win situation? Mudo wanted money. What did we want? It came down to a clean bathroom with shower, food, and security. Back and forth we discussed different options. Finally, we decided to let Mudo know in no uncertain terms we weren't just going to hand him money for one of his schemes. We would contribute only the cost of the new lock, duplicate keys, and a spigot for the shower. We also would propose turning Rich's *carraca* into a taco stand. We would contribute a total of five thousand pesos between all of us to get it ready. Mudo could reap steady profits as long as the food was good and the prices fair. He would be dependent on us as steady customers. If we weren't treated well, he would go out of business. We would tolerate no more extortion scams.

As we were wrapping up our talk, Sully burst in… furious.

"Whatever you got planned. I'm in, one hundred percent!"

All of us felt the anger in him. "What's going on?" I asked.

"They brought Enrique back. Butchers cut off his other leg. Went to Mudo's to get his guitar and they shined me on. Assholes!"

This was the final straw. We couldn't wait any longer. Together we headed straight to see Mudo. Our group seemed was growing and by the time we reached Mudo's *carraca* there were more than a dozen of us, including Chuy, Ramiro, and Tambor.

Gorilla, Nacho, Pepino, and Chico were all standing in front of Mudo's *carraca*. They seemed surprised and nervous at the size of our group.

Chico hurried into Mudo's *carraca* and soon the "big cheese" walked out. Gorilla stood ready with his club and we all knew about Nacho's switchblade. Didn't matter at this point.

I was one of two Americans who spoke fluent Spanish. The other, Scooter, was married to a Mexican woman and kept pretty much to himself. I was happy to see him come out and stand with us on this issue. His Spanish was peppered with the local slang. His wife's family was powerful, and Mudo knew it.

"Thanks for coming," I told Scooter. "You talk the talk the lingo better than I do, so you're the translator."

"Let's get it on" he said.

Randy started things off while Scooter translated. "We want the key to the lock that we already paid for."

Mudo looked at him hard and then surveyed all of us.

"One of you left it open at night and the lock was stolen. Your fault, not mine."

'Sounds like a crock of bullshit." said John.

"There's only one decision you have to make—the key or the money," Randy repeated.

Mudo hesitated and spit on the ground. "I'll think about it."

"Nothing to think about. Time is now!" Randy insisted.

Gorilla and Nacho stood on each side of Mudo. Club and switchblade ready. I could see this exploding any second.

"Hold on!... I think we can settle this in private. You and me, Mudo." Sully had moved next to Gorilla. Chuy and Yoshi stood on each side of Nacho. Q had my back. Mudo's eyes caught everything.

"Let's sit down inside your office and work this out." Better to help Mudo save face or it might get ugly. Some of those behind me were screaming for Enrique's guitar. They could soon be screaming for blood.

"Let them have Enrique's guitar. I have a proposal, I think you'll like."

I was hoping Mudo could see this was the only way to keep things from really getting out of hand and violent. As soon as I had mentioned Enrique's guitar, there was a chorus of loud roars from the group. Mudo had to know there was no bargaining on this issue.

"Why not," Mudo said calmly. He was no fool.

He brought out the guitar and Sully grabbed it, giving Gorilla a stare before walking away.

Mudo signaled me to follow him into the *carraca*. I asked Scooter to join us to make sure there was no misunderstanding.

I pulled out the paper with the written points we had agreed on and looked at Mudo.

"I want you to know, I didn't just draw this up. It was discussed and agreed to by all of us."

He gave a slight nod.

"First, the *baño*. We will pay the cost for a new lock and duplicate keys. Everything goes back to normal and we'll put a new spigot on the shower. Should be no more than five hundred pesos total."

Mudo spit on the ground. "Five hundred? *Muy poco*. What else?" he asked without agreeing.

"Here's where you make your money. You're asking for us to pay 500 pesos to "not" get transferred to Grande. I'll tell you right now nobody in our group is going to pay. If you did transfer them, you would lose a big source of money. I got them to agree to chip in and give you five thousand pesos for a taco stand. Rich's *carraca* would be perfect. You can own the business and make money and we would have a place to buy tacos. Everybody loves tacos. This way you make a steady profit and have cash coming in every day. What do you think?"

Mudo seemed more relaxed and was thinking. A smile was forming on his face.

"I might like your proposal. Let me think about it. As soon as I get the money for the new lock and keys, you can start using the *baño* again."

The three of us walked out together and shook hands. A resounding cheer greeted us. We had gotten over one big hurdle. No one knew what would come next.

A few days later I received a letter from my sister, Dinah. She wrote that Mike had lost his job, but it looked like Mom would be able to get a loan on the house. Promises had come from family members to chip in, but no money so far, only words. Mom was doing everything she could, even asking for help at the courthouse. I felt worse about what I was putting them through than my own situation. I could handle prison, but realizing the pain this was causing my family was unbearable. I had to figure something out.

The next day I was called to the visiting room and Jon was waiting for me. He looked serious, not wearing his usual smile. We embraced and I looked at him.

"What's up?"

"There's going to be a slight delay. Mel can't take you next."

"What happened?"

Jon cocked his head, "He's on a big case... *Goma*."

"*Goma*?"

"Gum. Opium."

I nodded, "For Mexican brown heroin."

"The farmers are getting smart down here. They've discovered they can make more money with opium than marijuana. It takes less space to grow and the farmers sell to the processors who make the heroin. It's easier to transport north to the border towns. Once it's processed, one kilo brings the same price as three hundred kilos of weed."

"Where's Mel now?"

"Where the action is, Culiacán . . . heroin capital of Mexico."

I smiled.

"What's so funny?"

"Our government puts the squeeze on Mexico to stop the marijuana traffic so the supply of heroin increases. Do the politicians really know what's going on?"

"No, and they're dealing with a killer. Not only the drug, but the Mexican mafia."

"Where would you put your money?"

"On Mel. He'll get the guy off."

"And in the meantime?"

"Be patient. You're next. He wants your case."

I smiled and shook his hand as he left.

I walked with the guard down the long dimly lit corridor to the entrance of *Correccionales*, kicking the floor as I went. The words "*manana*" and "just wait" were getting old. Everybody said to be patient. I wanted to yell...to scream! I needed to figure something out and actually do it.

October was drawing quickly to a close and the passing of each day had brought new developments. And changes. There was nothing I could really count on. The Mexicans were talking about hurricane season and the wild tropical storms that hit the coast. They expected one to hit us at any time.

"Last year," Chuy said, "the winds hit so hard the power went off and we were in total darkness. All we had for light were some candles and flashlights."

Jose paid me a visit and confirmed, "The rains are late this year, but they will come. Then you'll see God in all his might. Remember what happened to us last year?"

"Oh yeah, I had to walk through water up to my waist just to get back to my hotel. Did you make it home?"

"Almost, but I ran into a river in the streets and walked the rest of the way. Rosa was relieved to see me, then the electricity went out. A real mess."

I pushed the pad over to him and gave him my pencil.

"Draw me a map from here to the main road leading out of town."

"I know what you're thinking. I'll be ready for whatever you need." He drew a map and went over it with me. When he finished, I had a good idea how to get to the main road. From there, I knew how to find Jose's house.

"I may pay you a visit if the hurricane hits big like last year. Let Bill know we still might need Triumph Dave."

A new escape plan was taking shape in my mind. I thought Randy might want to join me.

"I don't like it," Randy said over dinner. "It's too risky."

"Living here is risky."

"But you have no guarantees. How can you plan?"

"By being ready when the time comes."

"And what if it doesn't rain. You could wait for a year. Or more."

"Not from what I've heard."

"O.K., Randy said, "so it rains. How the hell is a little rain going to get you out of here?"

"Not a little rain. I'm talking about a major storm. A hurricane."

"And you think the *Federales* are going to crawl into tree trunks like a bunch of bears, until it's over?"

"I'm talking about torrents of rain—and wind like you've never seen before. When the storm comes there's a good chance it'll knock the power out and maybe part of the wall. With no lights at night, they'd never spot us."

"Like I said, there are too many things you can't count on."

"Like what?"

"First you need a storm at night. Then it has to be so strong it cuts off the power. And you need to be sure the guards can't see you. When's the last time all those pieces fell into place at once?"

"Last year."

"There's one other point."

"I know."

"How do you get over the two walls?"

I stopped eating and stared at my plate. "A good question." Then I added, "If I can think of a way, would you be interested?"

"Interested in what?"

"Going with me."

Randy smiled.

"No guarantees, of course. Just be ready when the time comes."

He was thinking about it. "I'll let you know."

That evening, as I climbed into bed, I felt a burning sensation around my upper legs and genitals. I lowered my shorts and found colonies of red spots, small inflamed lumps that itched with the slightest touch. They hadn't been there earlier when I showered; I was always careful to stay clean. They had appeared so fast I thought an insect might have bitten me, possibly a spider. But these weren't bug bites, nor a prickly heat-type rash. These were sores. I showed Randy my legs and he smiled.

"Welcome to the club, brother. You can count on getting the "creeping crud" if you're here long enough. We all get it. You've got scabies."

"Scabies?"

"You get it from parasites."

"What's that mean?"

"They burrow under your skin and lay eggs."

"How do I get rid of it?"

"This is your lucky day. I still have some of my lotion left. It kills the critters, but takes a while."

"Hallelujah! I'll live," I said, as I looked at a big strawberry growing up my leg.

Randy didn't take long to make up his mind on my invitation to fly the coop. He had over four years left to serve on his sentence and I knew how bad he wanted to get home.

"I'm with you," he told me with certainty the next morning.

I set out to find a way to scale the walls. Since the tunnel attempt,

the Commission assumed it had carte blanche to the Americans'
quarters. Unannounced searches were conducted more frequently
than ever before. Nothing was safe and anything of value that was
openly displayed often found its way into Mudo's collection for
safe-keeping. Following Randy's lead, I began stuffing money in
cracks in the boards, into the toes of shoes that were wadded with
socks, and behind the gallery of surfing pictures that lined the
walls.

Our *carraca* had a loft, an area above the bunks where we
stored extra blankets and odds and ends, including the blender.
The loft was high, dark, and deep. Reaching it wasn't easy. I had to
stand up on a crate every morning to get the blender out. Anything electrical was in great demand and a blender would have
brought great rewards to a junkie. I used it to make fruit smooth-
ies that often served as breakfast for us.

One morning as I struggled to reach the blender, I almost fell
off the crate.

"There must be an easier way to do this," I said in disgust.

"Get a ladder," Randy answered.

Suddenly it hit me. "That's it!" I cried.

"What's it?"

"You're a genius," I told him.

"The ladder?"

"That's the answer!"

Randy leaned back on his bunk thumbing through a magazine.
"Gary and I thought about building one but decided against it.
Too much work for the few times we'd use it. But you're up there
every ..."

"It's the perfect excuse," I said, cutting him off. "We could build
it right under their noses and nobody'd question what we're
doing."

"Course not. Why should they?"

"They'd think it was for the loft, but it's our way out. Our way
over the walls."

Randy thought for a moment, then smiled. "Way to go bro."

I set out immediately to round up supplies. Finding lumber was no problem. Odd scraps of wood from broken cots and ongoing repair work were scattered everywhere. I was making my way back to the *carraca*, arms heavy with lumber, when Chico stopped me. He was full of questions. "What you doin weeth wood?" he asked.

"It's for our fireplace," I said sarcastically. "We're storing up for winter."

He laughed. "You funny. What you gringos making?"

"You're too smart for me, Chico. Can't fool you, can I?"

"No, you keep busy, huh?"

"Very busy," I said, starting to walk away. "Lots to do."

He stepped in front of me. "What you makeeng?"

"Glad you asked, Chico," I said, sounding somewhat troubled. "Maybe you can help."

His eyes lit up. "How?"

"Do you know anything about making ladders?"

"Makeeng ladders?"

"To climb up to our loft. Good idea, huh?"

"Sí. You pay me, I help." Curiosity satisfied, he walked away.

It took us a couple of days to get enough materials, but we were able to build a ladder in front of everybody. I climbed it daily for the blender and we both used it to store valuables up on the loft. Our normal routine did not seem suspicious at all.

# 9

## *Buried Alive*

The sun seemed to have disappeared and was replaced by a strange orange-grayness. The sky that had been blue and clear was now covered by clouds.

Just before dinner we were alerted that Hurricane Olivia was fast approaching. Time to change my clothes just in case. I dressed in my dark shirt and pants and stuffed Jose's map along with wads of money into the pockets. I was ready to go if the time came. Our nightly poker game helped us take our minds off the danger.

"Deal the fucking cards," Randy said nervously.

Barry sat cross-legged on the floor, his fingers calmly shuffling the deck. "Stay cool, man. It's just a friendly little game." He looked across the playing area to his partner, John, and smiled. "Or don't you dig the studs from Texas whippin' your ass?"

The games had become a contest between the states. Randy and I had beaten the two Texans consistently, but tonight was a different story. California was down five zip. My mind was on other things. So was Randy's.

"Like I always say," Barry taunted, "you can't keep cream from risin'. Class will tell."

Randy replied. "Sure bro, and the Texas two-step might help you cross the Rio Grande, but lord have mercy when the California wave comes your way."

Any other night I'd have followed through with a cheap shot or two. We worked to keep the rivalry active, giving meaning to an otherwise senseless pastime. I watched Barry deal the cards as I listened to the wind and rain slamming against the fragile dwelling.

It was impossible to judge the intensity of the storm from inside the *carraca*. Our small quarters had turned into an echo chamber. Rain pelted the sheet metal roofing with so much force that it sounded like a chorus line dancing overhead. The wind, finding its way through the seams, lifted and shook and whistled. Randy and I checked the light constantly. Dangling above, it swayed in the ever-changing air currents, creating eerie shadows.

The door suddenly flew open. Cosey rushed in; he was soaked. "She's a wild one," he said, wiping his face. "Any flooding in here?"

"So far so good," I answered.

"You're lucky," he told me. Then he turned to John. "You've got a small river running through your place. The rats are climbing the walls."

Barry shrugged.

"Too late now," John answered. "How's Enrique doing?"

"Sully carried him to one of the bunks. He's OK- dry at least."

"How bad is it out there?" I asked. "Could you see anything?"

Cosey removed his wet shirt and hung it on a nail. "Looks like a corner of the west wall's gone," he said. "I think some Mexicans are planning to go for it."

Not far away a piece of metal roofing ripped loose and crashed against something solid. I strained to hear follow-up sounds. There weren't any. No cries or shouts, no approaching footsteps. No way the guards could check out every disturbance on a night like this. We counted on that.

I jumped to my feet. "I'm going outside."

"But the lights," Randy said. "It's too soon."

"I have to see what's going on."

Cosey grabbed my arm. "What are you saying?"

"Randy and I are breaking out."

"You're what?" Barry said.

"We're hightailin it outta here. I have a map and I know where I'm going. Anyone wants to come, get ready!"

"Are you serious?" Cosey asked.

"I nodded, "All we need is a little more cooperation from Olivia."

A big gust of wind roared and the lights flickered off, on, and then off for good. John lit the candles.

I grabbed the ladder and moved toward the door, I could feel my body beginning to tremble. Adrenalin raced through my system. Calm down, I told myself, you're not going over now. I felt a queasiness in my stomach and wondered when I should make my move.

Randy was staring at me. "Well… you ready bro?"

I took a deep breath. "Ready," I repeated. "I'll check it out up top. Stay put until I come back for you."

"I'm coming with you. I'll steady the ladder." He followed me out the door.

Outside it felt like a wind tunnel. Torrents of air sucked through the narrow alleyway between shanties and made it nearly impossible for me to stand up. Water poured from the slanted rooftops like miniature Niagras mixing with the dirt and slime of the yard. The footing was treacherous.

We hooked the ladder over the edge of the roof. With Randy holding it tight below, I slowly began to climb through the waterfall to the top of the *carraca*. As I reached the top rung, I knew I had problems. How was I to step from the ladder onto the slippery corrugated roofing? I grabbed at anything I could to steady myself—sharp edges, torn scraps, bumpy ridges, even protruding nails. I couldn't raise up, let alone sit or stand. Spread-eagled on my belly, I strained to pull myself forward and lift my head as the gales of Hurricane Olivia slammed across Mazatlán at speeds of over 150 miles per hour.

Rain pelted my face, gouging my eyes. With my chin pressed hard against the roof I tried to look around. The power had gone off throughout the prison. No spark of light was visible anywhere through the dense curtain of water.

To my right was the north wall of the yard. Ahead, our escape route, the west wall. Cosey was right. A small corner had been blown away.

I tried to construct the escape plan. Randy and I would crawl across the rooftops to what remained of the first wall, climb over and race to its shorter twin, thirty feet beyond, dragging the ladder with us. From there it was over and out, free and clear.

My heart raced at the thought. The time had come. But how could we perform such acrobatics on a night like this? We'd be lucky to make it along the metal roofing without sliding off. My hopes now rested on more of the wall collapsing.

Further along, I spotted two dark shapes creeping on all fours toward the west wall. I couldn't see their faces, but I knew they weren't guards. Couldn't be sure, but one of them looked like Chuy. They had to be the escaping Mexican prisoners Cosey had mentioned.

A sudden gust of wind roared through the darkness. I dug my fingers into the wet metal grooves and heard an incredible roar. The upper portion of the wall was collapsing. A massive hole, at least twenty feet long, had opened before me. There was no doubt in my mind. It was time to make our move. I started back to tell the others.

Before I could reach the ladder, the entire compound was flooded with light. Generated by an auxiliary power source, two giant searchlights combed the yard, the roof-tops, and the walls. Teams of guards rushed to their positions, shooting helter-skelter

at anything that moved. Prisoners sloshed about the compound
trying to find cover. The circle of light pinpointed two would-be
escapees. They were now half-crouched, trying to work their way
to the open area of the broken wall. Guns exploded and bullets
whizzed across the yard. One of the men was hit, lurched back-
ward, and tumbled into the muck. As he fell, I caught a glimpse of
his face. It was Chuy.

A brick sailed toward the beam of light. It missed. Soon, dozens
of objects were being hurled through the soggy air towards the big
lights.

Bright sparks of gunfire showered the night as the beam moved
my way. I slid to the edge of the roof as the beam of light reached
me. There was no time. I dropped from the ledge into the fast-
moving torrent below, landing on my backside. As I hit, the
compound went partially dark and I heard a cheer. Someone had
thrown a winner. One light out. One to go.

Randy pulled me up and we returned to the *carraca*. I sat on
crate and contemplated my next move.

"What the hell's going on up there?" asked John.

I described the fury of the storm, the crumbled west wall, the
circle of armed guards—and Chuy.

"What do you think?" Randy asked.

"Don't want to walk into the bullets. Let's check it out. When
we see an opening, we move fast."

"You're right," John said. "Wait til it's safe."

Then we heard a loud rumble and the wall came tumbling down
right on top of us. I was completely buried as my whole life passed
before me in an instant. Total darkness. I couldn't see and I couldn't
move. I had no idea where anyone was. I yelled out over and over
again hoping someone could hear me through the thunderous storm.
Was everyone buried? Would I be found? I was paralyzed and the only
part of my body I could move, were two fingers on my left hand
sticking up through the rubble. Adrenaline was flowing through my
body and I still had my voice, loud and strong.

"Here, help, here" I screamed over and over again competing with the storm, gunshots, and moans of others. Soon I could hear voices in Spanish and English. I heard Randy call my name. He had an idea of where I was and could see my two fingers sticking out.

"We'll get you out Rob, don't worry. Move those fingers, if you can hear me." I wiggled them fast.

"Somebody help me," I heard Randy say as he started to pull the rubble and blocks off my body.

"Robert's down here," he yelled.

Someone pulled the bricks from my head and I could actually see again. The storm was swirling and I noted the top ten feet of the wall adjacent to our *carraca* was no longer there. No telling if the rest of the wall was going to collapse. Cosey and John were working fast with Randy to get me out, but I was stuck. A long and heavy steel beam was pinning me down and they couldn't get it off. It was crushing my legs.

They took off to find more help and returned with one of the *pila* supports to wedge beneath the beam. Twenty minutes later, my arms and chest were completely free of rubble, but the beam still rested on my legs. I saw Q and Sully with some of the Mexicans lending a hand. Three men were on the fulcrum and the others at the beam lifting, straining, pulling. Ever so slowly it inched upward. When it was just high enough, a space was cleared behind me and I was pulled out. I tried to get up, but my legs wouldn't cooperate. They wouldn't move.

I was lifted to a cot like a fragile piece of china, then raised into the air as outstretched arms carried me over the rubble. It was a rough journey. Midway across the yard the rotting fabric of the stretcher ripped and I hit the wet ground. The pain knifed through me. Randy hurried to find another cot and I was carried to the prison infirmary and placed on the floor with other injured prisoners.

The infirmary was crowded with sick and diseased prisoners, men who had arrived long before the storm swept across

Mazatlán. The dozen or so beds were all occupied. Even floor space was at a premium; wafer-thin mats clogged the walkways with bodies of the terminally ill. Now, emergency quarters had to be set up in the small adjoining anteroom to care for victims of the storm.

I was carried to this dim makeshift hospital room and placed on the damp cement floor next to Barry. Except for an old wooden desk, its top crowded with dusty medicine bottles, the room was devoid of furnishings. No blankets, no pads, no pillows.

The floor felt hard and cold. Careful as my friends were to set me down, I cringed with every motion. My body, caked with rubble, throbbed. Blood glistened from numerous cuts. And my left leg, with its ugly lump along the thigh, was bent in an unnatural way.

Randy knelt at my side to wipe some of the dirt and grime from my face.

"What's going to happen?" I asked in a thin voice. Breathing was difficult, talking almost impossible.

"You'll be fine," he said. "Don't worry."

"You shouldn't have done it," I said.

"Lie quiet. Don't talk."

"You shouldn't have stayed."

"Shhhh."

"You could be free. All you guys."

"Don't think about it."

"If it weren't for me, you'd be free." A jolt ripped through my body. I dug my fingertips into the palms of my hands.

"Don't try to talk," Randy said.

Then I passed out.

I was awakened by a bright light in my face. Someone was shaking me. "Wake up," a voice said.

"Leave him alone," someone said. "Don't touch him!"

The light went out. Randy, John and Cosey were standing over me pulling away a guard and his flashlight.

"He needs a doctor," John said. "And medicine."

The guard reached into his pocket and pulled out a paper. "This will help his pain. *Chiva.* Only fifty pesos."

"Where is the doctor?" Cosey asked.

"Everybody busy," the guard answered. "Many sick people."

Randy frowned. "Well, get one for chrissake. This man needs attention. Look at his leg."

Which leg? I wondered. They both hurt like hell—and what was wrong with them? Perhaps my condition was worse than I imagined.

Where's the doctor?

"With the injured," he answered.

"But these men are in pain," John said, pointing to me and Barry.

Then the warden arrived. "I brought medicine," In his hand he held a small bottle. "This should help until the doctor arrives."

The warden dropped two white tablets into my hand. Then he gave two to Barry. "Anyone else?"

Cosey stepped forward. His hands and arms were scratched and smeared with blood.

"What are those things?" Randy asked. "They look like aspirin."

The warden nodded. "Aspirin. Yes."

"My God!" John said. "Is that all you have?"

"We are low on supplies. This emergency came at a bad time."

"God have mercy. You might as well be passing out Milk Duds."

The warden stepped out into the corridor, ignoring John's remark. He returned with four armed guards. "Everyone not injured come with me."

"Where?" Cosey asked.

"You'll stay with the others in the library until the storm has ended." He turned, motioning to those who could follow.

Randy started to leave. "Hang in there," he told me, "you'll be fine."

"Be strong," Cosey added. "And don't worry."

The room was emptying. John was on his knees thanking the

Lord for saving our lives. When he stood to leave, there were tears in his eyes.

Only Barry and I remained. He had stretched out on the floor again and was asleep. I closed my eyes and the room began spinning. I wanted to get up and move, to shake the throbbing from my head and body. But my legs were useless, my arms were weak and my mind was being invaded by grotesque images.

I stared at the ceiling as a stranger crouched over me. He was wearing a shredded hospital gown and in his right hand he carried a huge knife, its blade jagged and dirty. He took my left leg in his hand and squeezed the flesh like Silly Putty, then drew a line around my upper thigh with his fingernail leaving a trail of blood. Now he lowered the blade of his knife and buried it deep in my leg. Ayyyyyy…

I opened my eyes and the man disappeared. Perspiration rolled down my face; my hands were clammy. Was he a vision of things to come?

I dwelled on the macabre, knowing my leg was certainly broken and possibly mangled. And what about the other one? I couldn't move it either.

The doctors here aren't the best in the world, I told myself. Cut first, talk later was their credo. I pictured myself with one leg. Then with no legs. Enrique's image flashed before me.

I breathed deeply, filling my lungs with dank air. Then I prayed, unaware that the wind and rain had begun to subside.

Morning came, and the sun was streaming through the windows of the infirmary as I came to. There was a short Mexican standing at my feet staring down at me. "Who are you?" I asked.

"*Medico,*" he answered.

The stranger looked too young to be qualified for medical work. But he wore a white doctor's jacket over his shirt and slacks and had a stethoscope dangling around his neck. "Do you have anything for pain?" I asked.

He shook his head, 'What is wrong?"

"My legs. I can't move them."

His eyes traveled quickly over my body. Then he disappeared for a few minutes. When he came back, he was carrying a flat piece of wood and a roll of tape. "Here," he said, handing me his handkerchief, "put this in your mouth and bite. It will help."

"What do you mean?"

He didn't answer. Instead, he ripped away the leg of my Levi's. I cried out.

My scream didn't faze him. He placed the piece of wood under my left calf and began wrapping it with tape.

"No!" I yelled. "Stop!"

Barry sat up straight. "What hell are you doing to him?"

I gritted my teeth. It didn't help.

"You idiot," Barry shouted. "That's not where his leg's broken. It's his thigh. Can't you see the bone sticking out?'

He glanced at the upper part of my leg. His eyes stayed on the massive protrusion only an instant before he walked away.

It wasn't much later when Randy poked his head into the room. "Good morning," he smiled.

"How did you get here?" Barry asked.

"I came to check things out. How's it going?"

"Do you have the run of the prison or something?"

Randy shook his head. "I slipped Mudo a few pesos."

I raised my hand a few inches and Randy took it. Then he squatted on the floor.

"I see a doctor's been here," he said.

"Some doctor," Barry snickered.

"Look where he put the splint," I said.

"He didn't even look at me," Barry said, disgusted. "The turkey couldn't get out of here fast enough."

"You'll be OK. Both of you. Just hang tough for a little while."

"What about the others?" I asked. "Any problems last night?"

Randy frowned. "Not if you don't mind sleeping with your nose up a stranger's butt. That library was so crowded. I'm sure I've got crabs in my eyebrows."

"Did anybody get over the wall?"

"Six Mexicans are missing."

"Any of us?"

"All accounted for."

"Randy?"

"Yes."

"I don't know what's going to happen to me but they may put me out if they operate . . ."

"They'll fix you up. You'll be fine."

"That's not what I meant. I have money and the escape map on me for the trip we were taking." I reminded him. "Don't want them to find it. Empty my pockets and take my shoes. I won't be using them for a while."

"Good idea. Forgot about that." He pulled the map and some pesos out of my pocket and grabbed my shoes. "I'll be waiting for you."

Randy stood and walked toward the door, then turned to face Barry and me once more. "Hang in there," he said. Then he was gone.

That afternoon two ambulance attendants in police uniforms arrived with a stretcher and went directly into the infirmary. A few minutes later they carried out a Mexican whose chest was heavily taped. They returned shortly.

"*Dónde está* Roberto Miller?" one asked.

"Here," I answered.

The attendants lifted me into the stretcher without explanation and took me to a cement slab outside CPM's main entrance. There, I was laid next to the Mexican with the bandaged chest. The two of us remained alone and unguarded for the next half hour.

The Mexican's name was Julio. He had been imprisoned in the Grande section. His ribs were broken and he had pneumonia as well. He coughed and wheezed and gurgled. Like me, he was unable to budge.

Julio had no idea where we were being taken or what to expect. Even after we were loaded onto gurneys and placed in an ambulance, our destination remained a mystery.

For the next fifteen minutes we were treated to a bumpy, agonizing ride over water-soaked and muddy roads. Except for a few lingering clouds, the sky was clear; but Olivia was far from a memory. Trees were uprooted everywhere. Many houses of the poor had been flattened; those of the more affluent still stood, but they were roofless or devoid of doors and windows. Water churned across the most unlikely places—lawns, sidewalks, school yards—seeking an outlet to the sea. Driverless automobiles teetered on their sides and roofs hundreds of feet from the nearest avenues. Only the major hotels, those concrete and steel towers of tourism, had escaped with minimal damage.

The ambulance pulled to a stop in front of the sagging Hospital Civil. With its blown-out windows, it looked like a relic from World War II.

Julio went first. I followed, wheeled in on the gurney, flanked by the two attendants and a set of guards. We traveled clear around the building, down corridors that reeked of ether, urine, and stale bodies, ending up at the caged prison ward.

Julio was in bed on a bare mattress when I reached the room. Two other beds were occupied by men I had never seen before. They were from a prison on one of the islands off the pacific coast and were scheduled for surgery within the next few days.

The lone empty bed was mine. I was too tired, too weak and too crippled with pain to notice that the crumpled sheet the attendants set me on was crawling with ants.

The next thing I knew a pretty young lady in white was standing over me sticking a needle into my arm. Her name was Miss Moreno.

"What are you giving me?" I asked.

She withdrew the needle quickly and pressed a piece of cotton over the puncture in the skin.

"Valium," she answered as she looked about the room. I got the impression she didn't like being locked up with four undesirables.

"Valium?" I repeated.

Miss Moreno stopped at the door. "It will help you sleep." Then she tapped for the guard to let her out.

"I have to go to the bathroom," I said.

She misunderstood me. "The toilets are not working since the storm."

The door opened and she hurried out. I wet the bed.

Miss Moreno returned frequently to give me shots. On one occasion she was accompanied by an older, rather distinguished looking gray-haired man who identified himself as Dr. Arriaga. He seemed anxious and stayed just long enough to glance at my leg and shake his head in a sorrowful way. The dirt that covered my skin and cement that caked my hair failed to move the hospital staff.

As time passed, I became more and more lethargic. I lived in a fog, yet was still aware that the conditions surrounding me were despicable, especially for a hospital. Besides not being changed and lying in my own excrement, I hadn't even been offered food or water.

I soon learned that patients in the prison wards were virtually helpless. Few services were given and requests almost always ignored. The only way I could care for my needs was to remain perfectly still. My mattress became my world, all purpose, all serving—one I shared with the growing community of ants who doted on my incapacity.

If I retained any spark of determination it was due to the presence of Julio. As I grew weaker, he grew stronger. He tried his legs with short walks about the room, first to the foot of his bed, then to a window several yards beyond. Walking to the window became a ritual. Soon Julio was hesitating before heading back. His stops became longer as he lingered to study the metal grill that stretched across the window and the path outside. At night, he stood coughing and sniffling at the window, his head turned toward the door as if testing the guard for a reaction.

On the fourth morning I mumbled Julio's name and he came to my side. I wanted to know how far we were from the ground.

"A very short drop," he said in Spanish. "We're on the first floor."

"Take me with you," I pleaded in a slow, breathy voice.

Julio frowned. "What do you mean?"

"I know what you're going to do," I said. "Can you take me with you?"

He looked at me, then at the door, then at me again. "How?"

"Carry me."

"Impossible."

"I can't do it alone." The words choked in my throat.

"Too dangerous," he sniffed, shaking his head. "Bad enough for one to go."

"You're right. But I'd crawl on my hands and knees to get out of here."

Julio returned to the window for a few minutes then walked slowly back to his bed.

That afternoon, as I lay staring into space, I felt a hand touch my shoulder. I turned to see a man in a white suit standing by the edge of the bed.

"I am Dr. Guzman," he said. "Vice-Consul Parker asked me to look in on you. Just lie still while I examine your leg." He stepped around the foot of the bed to the other side. When he had seen enough, he came forward again.

"In time, your right leg should heal by itself. The other leg, however, looks very bad. The splint is doing no good. It is on the wrong bone."

I nodded my head slightly.

"The femur is broken quiet severely. The leg should be set and put in traction. You should know that you could be bedridden for a year or more waiting for the bone to heal—if it ever does. You stand a better chance of walking again with an operation. A steel pin inserted in your leg would speed the healing process greatly. I feel an operation is necessary, but we must have permission to proceed. I'll discuss the matter with Dr. Arriaga and Vice-Consul Parker."

The doctor departed, leaving Miss Moreno behind. She was preparing to give me another injection. The doctor's voice haunted me. "Chance of walking again . . . operation." No! I would not stay in this lousy, stinking, crawling hole for a year. If I were to maintain my sanity, I needed help. I had to get out of this place.

# 10

## *Visitors*

The sweet smell of flowers reached my consciousness. I was suddenly whirling through a technicolor fantasy of blossoms-lavender, plumeria, pinks, ginger—far from the black dreams that haunted me. Something soft brushed against my cheek and I opened my eyes, slowly. My vision was blurred, but I didn't have to focus to know someone very special was close. It was her perfume, her touch, her voice as she pressed her face to mine and spoke my name.

My heart seemed to explode, clogging my throat. It was all I could do to mouth the word, "Mom."

For the next few minutes neither of us could speak. Tears filled my eyes as I held tight—and for the first time in months I knew what it was like to feel safe and secure.

"I'm so glad you're here," I said.

"Dinah got a phone call last night, and then called me. Some woman ... I think her name was Gretchen." One hand clung to mine, "We came as fast as we could."

We? I was so taken at seeing my mother I hadn't noticed anyone else. Now a familiar face, partially covered by dark shaggy hair and a bushy beard, came into view. It belonged to my cousin, Bill.

"Are they giving you pain medication?" Mom asked. The smile on her lips could not mask the concern in her eyes.

"Valium," I answered.

She put her hand to my forehead. "He has a fever," she told Bill. Smoothing my hair, she stopped, fingering a hard substance. "What's this stuff?"

"Cement. I've been picking it out for days."

Bill's eyes narrowed as he brushed cement from the grainy sheet. "What about X-rays?" he asked.

I moved my head slowly from side to side. "I haven't moved from this bed since they brought me here."

"What do you mean?"

"I'm a prisoner." My lips were dry and cracked. I moistened them with my tongue.

Mom checked the small table near my bed. "There isn't even any water. Who takes care of you?"

"Julio," I answered, turning to the far bed. "He gets me water. And a nurse comes in once in a while."

Her body grew tense. "Has she ever bathed you? It looks like you've had that shirt on a month. Smells like it too. She touched the corner of a small blanket that covered me.

"And this needs washing. It's all stained."

"It's fine. Don't touch it."

Mom ignored me. "I want to see your leg." She rolled back the blanket, exposing my left leg and the brown mess that escaped my shredded jean.

"My God!" she cried, stunned by her first sight of my disaster area. She regained her composure, straining for objectivity.

"Your leg's crooked. It's skewing inward!" She continued to stare, taking inventory, her jaw set tight. "And doesn't anyone ever bring you a bedpan for chrisssakes? What the hell do they do around here?" Her voice was beginning to quaver.

Bill squeezed her arm. "Let's get him cleaned up. Then we'll talk to that doctor."

"God only knows what condition his leg is in," she said.

Bill moved to my side. "You won't be in this zoo much longer cousin," he told me. "This could be your last day."

"What?"

"Barbara and I saw the Vice-Consul on our way here from the airport to try and get you deported."

"Parker?"

"He said he had his own doctor look in on you. Right?"

I nodded. "Dr. Guzman."

"A court hearing is set for tomorrow morning. The judge will be asked to sign an order having you transferred to a private hospital . . . one with facilities to operate."

"Judge? Court?"

"We can't get you moved without an order," Mom said. "It's just a formality." Her expression was less confident than her voice.

"What about deporting me?"

"I phoned the State Department this morning, with no results. I couldn't wait for results—couldn't wait for anything—I had to get here. A Mr. Wauk said they'd investigate, send a cable. And Parker . . . well ... he just brushed my words aside and started talking about the doctor."

"Deportation seems to be a dirty word around here," Bill said. "We'll work that out later. The most important thing is to get you healthy again, cousin."

"Now," Mom asked grimly, "where's some water?"

I pointed to the small area behind a plastic curtain. She disappeared briefly, returning with several old towels and a flat pan sloshing with discolored liquid, her face hard with anger.

"This is really some great hospital," she said, with sarcasm.

Bill raised an eyebrow.

"The toilet hasn't been flushed since God knows when. I just tried and it backed up. The floor's covered with . . ." She made a face and set the bowl on the bed table.

I held out my hand.

"We'll get you cleaned up. But we'll have to cut those pants off you."

I reached for the bowl of water.

"Just lie back," Bill said. "We'll do the work."

"Water," I said. "I'm thirsty."

"Then hang on," he answered. "I'll get some fresh."

I took the bowl and brought it to my lips. "This is OK," I said.

"No!" Mom yelled, taking it from my hands. "It's full of sediment—probably every disease in the book."

"But it's all there is," I told her. "And my mouth's like cotton."

She set the bowl down and went for her purse to find a roll of mints.

"Try these for now," she said, placing one on my tongue.

She started to set the rest in my hand when she spotted a trail of ants. She gasped and drew back. "Bill look ... the bed's alive!"

Bill hurried to the door and banged on the bars. "I want a clean sheet, some towels and a pair of scissors," he demanded of the guard.

The man in blue shrugged his shoulders and walked away. He came back with Miss Moreno.

Bill repeated his list to the nurse. A few minutes later she passed everything but the scissors to him through the openings between the steel bars. "Didn't you forget something?" he asked.

"No," she answered. "No scissors."

"Well, what do you have that's sharp?"

She shook her head. "Nothing."

"Can you use this?" Julio asked from across the room, holding up a razor. "It is rusty but it works." He would have brought it over, but his broken ribs now pained him so badly he was bedridden.

Bill unscrewed the blade from its holder then he and Mom began the unenviable task of freeing me from my excrement-filled pants. They worked first on the right side, slicing and slashing through the soggy denim from the waistband on down. They then moved to the other side and repeated the process. The slightest twist or turn sent shockwaves through my body. The valium may have made me groggy, but it did nothing to ease the pain.

"Jesus Christ!" Bill bellowed as my shitty pants were finally free and Mom began to pull the cloth away from my skin. The smell was unbearable. The sight must have been even worse.

Mom stuffed the pants, or what was left of them, into a plastic bag, knotting the top, and tossed it on the floor.

"I'm keeping these. "Plaintiff's exhibit one". And if there's any delay in getting you out of here, I'll shove them in Parker's face."

Then she hurried behind the plastic curtain to wash her hands. When I saw her again, she had rolled up the cuffs of her slacks and was taking the curtain divider down. "Help me slip this under him," she said to Bill.

For the next half hour Mom washed excrement from my hips and buttocks, working extra carefully around the sore left side. The rinse water seemed never to be clean, no matter how often Bill changed it. Finally, when she could do no more, exhausted with the emotional drain of horror and anger, she asked Miss Moreno for some ointment to rub on my sensitive skin.

"What are these things?" Bill asked pointing to a spatter of dark red spots.

"I couldn't get it all," Mom answered. "What's left will have to wear off. At least he's cleaner." Bill picked at one of the crusty pieces. It began to bleed. "This isn't dried shit," he said. "It's a scab. What the hell's he got?"

I didn't want to tell them about the scabies. As far as I was concerned, they were the least of my problems. I pointed to my left heel instead. "It's sore," I said.

Mom squeezed some ointment on her fingers and began rubbing around the heel and tendon. "No wonder," she said. "The bandage has cut into your skin."

"I have a few things to tell Dr. Guzman when I see him." She replaced the top on the tube. Then she had Bill lift me gently while she pulled the soiled sheet and plastic from under me. She replaced them with clean bedding.

"The nurse said I should get some Pampers. Or paper diapers."

"You should get some Pampers? Does she think you have in and out privileges?" Mom shot a dirty look toward the barred door then checked her watch. "It's time to see Dr. Guzman." She picked up her purse as Bill started to follow. "I'll go alone," she told him. "You stay here with Robby."

Bill nodded. "Be careful."

She nodded back. Then she kissed me and was gone.

My head was spinning and my body ached from all the activity. I wanted to sleep but that was impossible. I watched Bill as he lumbered nervously in front of the window, one shoulder lower than the other. It wasn't that he carried the weight of the world on his right side, he just walked that way. He always did.

"Barbara's off," he said finally. "She just got into a cab."

"What's she going to see Guzman for?" I asked.

"To get some questions answered. Parker set up the appointment."

"About the operation?"

He nodded. "And getting you transferred. He's the one who talks before the judge tomorrow. His testimony's going to get you out of here."

I took a deep breath. "God, I hope you're right."

"The judge has no choice."

"Really?"

"You need the operation and they can't do it here. It's as simple as that."

I closed my eyes. "Billy?"

"What?"

"Go see Felix and Jose and let them know where I'm at as soon as I get transferred to the other hospital. I'm going to figure something out. I was ready to go when that wall came tumbling down on me."

"Will do, they were already on my list."

"I'm sorry."

"For what?"

"I just shit in bed again."

It was almost two hours before Mom returned. She was toting a big paper bag, the type with handles. "I've been shopping," she announced. She pulled out a large bottle of fresh water, a bar of soap, paper diapers, a toothbrush and toothpaste, and some fruit. "Damn," she said, "I forgot a cup and washrags."

"We'll get that stuff later," Bill said. "Tell me about Guzman."

She busied herself with her purchases as she talked, placing a paper diaper between me and the second clean sheet Bill had procured.

"I liked him. And I trust him. He got his medical degree in the U.S. so there was no language barrier. He gave me three choices: Robby can have surgery in a private hospital with modern facilities for eight hundred to one thousand dollars—and I think that's more than fair; or he can have the operation here—god forbid! — for half the price. Or...he can have no operation at all and just rot in this filth for a year or so."

"Guess which choice I took?" Mom plopped down in a chair, combing her damp hair with her fingers. "God, it's hot."

I had to know. "Do you have enough money?"

"I'm loaded. I brought every dollar we had stashed away for attorney fees." She pulled her shoulders back. "Haven't you noticed my new figure?"

I hadn't, but now I really looked at Mom. She was still pretty, but her once full cheeks were hollowed—and her clothes bagged. She'd lost a lot of weight and was almost skinny, everyplace but her bust. That area was a good facsimile of Marilyn Monroe.

"I had a heck of a time balancing them. Dollars on one side, fiber fill on the other." She was up again, "Where's a glass?" finding one on a neighboring table, retreating into the alcove to scrub it. "What about the hearing?" Bill asked.

"It's set for nine-thirty in the morning. We're to be there when Dr. Guzman testifies." Mom opened the bottled water and filled the glass, placing it in my hand. "Don't drink any other water," she commanded.

I drank thirstily while they talked.

"And the transfer?" Bill insisted.

"Dr. Guzman said the judge might not sign the order until Saturday. That would mean two more days of this."

"Why the delay?"

She rolled her eyes toward the ceiling. "Who knows? Apparently, the judge takes his own sweet time."

"OK, we wait," Bill said. "Then what?"

Mom walked slowly toward the window and stared out. "Someone named Arriaga will perform the surgery; Guzman will assist."

"Who's Arriaga?" Bill asked.

"Head of orthopedics here at Hospital Civil," Mom answered.

Bill threw his hands up. "That's some terrific reference."

"Guzman said he's an excellent surgeon, one of the finest down here. He operated on Guzman's wife last year."

"Well, that raises all sorts of questions. How did Guzman feel about his wife at the time? Is she still alive? Has . . ."

"Bill, stop it!" Mom said sharply. "The point is, we have no choice. Right now, all I care about is getting Robby out of here and into a private hospital with X-ray facilities and decent care." She looked tired.

Bill nodded. "I'm sorry, Barbara. You're right." He held her for a moment. "What do you say we get out of here for a while. You could probably use a bite to eat and some rest."

Mom thought for a second before agreeing. She carried the pan into the alcove, then returned to my side. "Do you need anything else before we go?"

Anything else? I had all I needed. I had my family. And they were fighting for me. "Nothing else, Mom. Just come back."

She smiled. "We'll be back a little later—after dinner."

"They won't let you in," I told her. "Not at night. The electricity's still off."

"Then we'll be back in the morning, right after the hearing. And with good news." She put her hand to my forehead. "It's still hot," she told Bill. "I swear he has a fever."

Bill took Mom's arm and led her to the door. "I'll bring a razor," he said, "and clean your face." Then he banged on the bars. "We're leaving," he told the guard.

Mom turned for one last look. I raised my hand as high as I could and waved. Then my eyes brimmed with tears.

Gretchen came to see me first thing in the morning on her way to visit Cosey. She carried magazines and a parcel wrapped with brown paper and cord.

"I talked with your sister the other night," she said. "I had to let your family know what had happened to you." She looked apprehensive, afraid I might be angry at her for causing alarm.

I took her hand and said, "Good things are in the works, thanks to you." I told her about my mother and Bill being in town and how they were working to get me transferred to a private hospital for an operation on my leg.

"Everyone'll be so glad to hear that," she smiled. Her expression changed abruptly. "They need good news."

*Correccionales* was still a disaster area, she told me. The prisoners were without water and surviving on oranges and food brought in by outsiders.

"They're trying to rebuild the *carracas* using whatever scraps they can find. Until they do, they're sleeping in the open on the ground. Everything's gone. All their possessions, everything." Gretchen took a deep breath.

I was afraid to ask, but I had to know.

"Have you heard anything about Enrique?"

Gretchen hesitated, "He didn't make it. They found him under some rubble."

I closed my eyes and could see him strumming the guitar. I could almost hear his voice. Tears were running down my cheeks.

"Give me a sec."

Gretchen walked over and gently touched me.

I took a deep breath and we were both still for a few minutes. Gretchen wiped my eyes with a cloth.

"Anything else," I finally asked.

"Randy asked me to give you this." She set the parcel down. "It's your shoes and papers."

"I hope I'll be needing them."

"Is your mother coming in today?"

"When the hearing's over."

"I want to meet her," Gretchen said. "Very much."

"Then come back. Please."

"I will," she said. "And if you need anything, just let me know."

"Just one thing" I told her. "Tell everyone to hang tough."

Gretchen nodded, then smiled. "You got it."

It was nearly noon when Bill arrived. He had come ahead to let me know the transfer had been approved. Mom was staying behind to sign the papers.

"The judge took one look at Barbara and turned on. Either that, or we caught him in a good mood."

"When do they move me?"

"Today. Just as soon as they can get a few cops off emergency duty to ride with you. They're a little short-handed since the storm."

I clenched my fists. "Awright!"

"Hey, I picked up some food for you," Bill said. "I hope you're hungry."

My stomach was still upset, but I was noncommittal.

"And I brought a clean t-shirt and the razor. We'll get you fixed up."

Bill's mealtime offering was a fried shrimp dinner he had picked up at the Shrimp Bucket. The smell made me queasy, but I ate two shrimp anyway. Bill finished the rest.

By the time Mom arrived I was nauseous. As the afternoon passed and it grew darker, I became depressed. No one had come to take me away. We didn't even know where I was to go.

"You should be gone by now," Mom said, lighting a cigarette. "What's taking so long?"

"Nobody's coming," I said. "That's the way they operate. Always *mañana*."

She threw the matches down. "They'd better come—and while there's still enough light to get you out of here."

"I wonder if Parker knows anything?" Bill asked.

Mom took a long drag on her cigarette. "Dammit," she snapped. "I'm going to call him. The court order specifically states- immediate transfer."

"The Consulate is probably closed by now and besides, these phones aren't working," Bill said.

"The hell they're not," Mom corrected. "I saw a medic talking on one when I came in. And I have Parker's home phone number." She called for the guard and stormed out, promising not to return until she got results.

It was a good half hour before we saw her again. It was dark outside and the bleakness of the hospital's room and corridors was mellowed by candlelight. She seemed exhausted, drained of the momentum that had propelled her earlier. "It looks like you'll be here one more night," she said.

I didn't comment. I just stared wide-eyed at the ceiling.

"Parker said something about being short-handed."

"Now when?" Bill asked.

"First thing in the morning."

"For sure?"

Mom reached into her purse and pulled out a small glass vial. "He promised," she said, shaking two tablets into her palm. Then she set them near my bottle of water. "Take one if you're restless tonight."

"What are they?" I asked, not even looking.

She closed her purse. "Sleeping pills."

I was dead to the world when Mom and Bill arrived the next morning. When I finally awakened, Mom was staring at me. She was smoking one of her inevitable cigarettes. I asked her for water, then an apple from the supply of fruit she had brought the day before.

The next minute the guard was unlocking the door and Mr. Parker was standing in our midst explaining, "The court order for your transfer to a private hospital was taken to the warden yesterday, but somehow the City Police never received a copy."

Mom straightened. "I have a copy of the order in my purse," she said. "Give it to the police."

"I'll get everything straightened out," Parker said. "It shouldn't take long. I just wanted you to know the reason for the delay." He forced a smile and was gone.

By eleven Mom had rolled up her pants and visited the rest-room twice while her smoke wafted out the window in a continuous billow. It was now almost twenty-four hours since the order for immediate transfer had been signed.

"I can't wait around like this," she said, finally. "I have to find out what's going on."

"Where you going now?" Bill asked.

"Where else?" she shrugged. "To call Parker ... to see if he's found out anything."

When Mom returned, she was tense and angry. "He wasn't there. We just have to wait. Damn!"

Her backside smacked the chair and Bill wiped his brow and unbuttoned his shirt. It was hot and humid in the crowded room. The window was open wide, but no air was circulating. He let out a deep sigh.

I closed my eyes as Mom said, "I should take a tranquilizer, but I'm not going to."

Then I heard her begin to chant. "Om Shanti, Om Shanti, Om Shanti" She had taken up Yoga and meditation several years before, when she was trying to quit smoking. It didn't help then and it didn't help now. "Enough!" she said suddenly springing up. "I'm going to the Consulate and have a nervous breakdown."

I looked at her and grinned, "Good," I said.

"I'll crack up all over their goddamn floor, if necessary, but I'm not leaving there until I know you've been transferred. And I'm taking your shitty pants with me." She snatched the bag with its ugly contents from under the bed and called for a guard. I was smiling as she disappeared; something was being done!

I didn't see Mom again for nearly three hours. By then I was across town in a private room.

# 11

## Sanatorio Mazatlan

Centered between the beach and the heart of the city, five minutes in either direction, I found a new home—the sprawling Sanatorio Mazatlán. A Catholic hospital, immaculate inside and out. Nursing nuns, spotless and crisp in ankle-length uniforms, moved eagerly along glossy corridor floors. Even the air smelled pure. Fresh-cut flowers in imaginative arrangements were spotted at random in public places. The atmosphere was impressive, particularly after a stint at Hospital Civil.

I was wheeled in on the gurney from the ambulance to Room 22, private quarters across from the nurses' station near the main entrance. No sooner was I settled in bed—a real hospital-type bed that raised and lowered—than Mom, looking frazzled, appeared in the doorway.

"You finally made it," she sighed with relief.

Vice-Consul Parker was with her; he'd driven her to this new hospital himself. He stayed just long enough to nod to me and accept Mom's hand and thanks. A mock salute and he was gone.

I motioned for Mom to sit and relax. Instead, she moved quickly to survey the room.

She opened a door. "You have a closet. And look . . . two pillows." She found another door and stepped inside. I heard the sound of rushing water. "A toilet," she exclaimed, "and it works!"

She spotted a sofa across from my bed. "I can sleep here. Parker said it would be all right." Then she paused, hands on hips, and smiled, "This is certainly a contrast from that pig pen." I started to agree, but she interrupted. "Did they X-ray your leg?"

"Yes. They stopped on the way over."

Mom glanced around the room again, then moved to the entrance, stuck her head out, and peered up and down the hall. She turned and faced me. "Where's Bill?"

"He took off," I said.

"Off where?"

"He's around here someplace, checking things out."

"What things?" And sensing danger, "What's wrong?"

"Nothing."

She nodded, but not at my words. She was reading behind them. She reached for a cigarette and struck a match. It flared as Dr. Guzman poked his head through the doorway.

The doctor glanced first at Mom, then at me. "How are you both doing now?"

"Much better. This is quite an improvement," Mom answered.

"We've scheduled the necessary tests for this afternoon. The operation is planned for tonight or tomorrow morning."

Not much later an aide appeared with a tray of food. Mom raised an eyebrow. "It looks like they won't be taking you tonight," she said. "They don't usually feed a patient before surgery." Then she sighed. "Maybe they're trying to build up your strength first."

I ate. And ate. Good thing too, for as the afternoon progressed, I needed all the energy I could muster. First a nurse came to take blood. She was followed by another wanting a urine sample. Then more blood tests, shots, and a transfusion for my internal bleeding. By the time Bill returned I had been poked, jabbed, and probed from every angle —and had been bathed from head to toe and dressed in a clean hospital gown.

"There's one guard right outside your door," he said in a low voice, "and another one across the street opposite that window." Bill walked to the window and examined the frame. "It shouldn't take much to knock this out. If we could get rid of the guard, you could make it. Easy."

"Sounds good," I answered.

Mom stared in disbelief. "What the hell are you guys talking about?" It was obvious she knew what we were talking about—her voice was rising, trembling. "You just got here."

"We've got to make plans," I told her calmly.

"But I prefer legal. Can't we go legal?"

Bill answered, "You know he can only stay here four days. Then it's back to Hospital Civil or CPM. Is that what you want?"

"No, No! But I'll talk to the doctor. He'll get us more time—I know he will."

"I won't go back, Mom. I'll do anything to get out. Anything. And at any time."

Mom was still. Her expression was unfathomable. I waited for her reaction.

"You're right." She drew a deep breath. "I've been a fool. I was so happy about the transfer I actually forgot about tomorrow—all the tomorrows."

She glanced at the frosted glass of the window, then back to me. "I'll do everything I can to help. And we'll try every way—legal— illegal—anything to get you out of here."

Dr. Arriaga entered, holding a large manila envelope. He had seen the X-rays. He placed the envelope on my bedside table. He would operate at noon tomorrow, straighten the bone and insert a steel rod to strengthen and hold the bone in place. There should be no difficulties.

As soon as he left, we scanned the X-rays. My femur was in two parts, the upper portion dropping at least one inch below the top of the lower portion, a thorn-like splinter on the outer side. That bone would never have healed without surgery.

I heard Mom muttering, "Plaintiff's exhibit two."

I was offered no food that evening, nor the next morning when the food cart rolled past my door. "They'll be coming to prep you for surgery," Mom said. But the morning dragged slowly on and no one appeared.

Just before noon a nurse entered holding a hypodermic needle. She didn't use it. She simply wandered in, then out. Shortly after, a gurney was wheeled in by a large man in green surgical garb who motioned for Mom and Bill to leave the room. The next thing I knew strong arms were sliding under me and I felt myself lifted away from the bed. Mom rushed in to find me strapped to the wheeled convenience.

"What are you doing to him?" she shouted.

If the man understood English, he paid no attention. I was rushed past her, into the hall and away.

We turned a corner and two double doors swung shut. A nurse was waiting with a needle, ready to bury it in my skin. Whatever displeasure her needle caused was offset by her striking good looks, a light skinned refined beauty. Her name, she said, was Esperanza de los Angeles, which meant "Hope of the Angels." I took it as a good omen. I told her that Los Angeles was close to home and mumbled about the coincidence when the injection began to take effect. As my eyes closed, I could see her smiling. I told myself I was in good hands.

When I awoke Esperanza was still at my side. I knew nothing about the operation, only that my left leg was entombed in plaster and without feeling. Soon I was back in my room, fully awake and trembling with cold. Mom tried to warm me, first by rubbing my hands, then by covering me with the bedspread. It didn't help. The only other thing she could find was the soiled blanket that came with me from Hospital Civil.

A nurse walked in and became outraged. "*La cobija está sucia*," she ranted. "*La cobija está sucia*." She pulled the dirty blanket away, tossed it back in the closet and left.

Mom pulled it out once more. "What's her problem?"

"She's upset because the blanket is filthy."

"Right now, I don't give a damn," Mom said with a toss of her head. She was about to spread the old blanket over me again when the nurse reappeared carrying a fresh one.

A second nurse followed closely behind with a stand, tubes and a plastic bag of dark red blood. She hesitated before inserting the needle in my vein.

The shivering grew progressively worse. My teeth began to chatter. Mom pressed her body against my chest, trying to warm me. She yelled, "Bill! Get help!"

He brought back a man in green cotton clothes who summoned a nurse. She gave me a shot in the rump, which had no effect. A second shot was administered in my arm. I calmed down only briefly. One more injection, this time in my hip, brought relief. I slept.

When I came to, I was surrounded by a trio of nurses. One was jabbing my arm with a needle while the others were setting up another stand on which to dangle a bottle of clear liquid. Now I had tubes running into both sides and I was wringing wet. Perspiration ran from my face, my neck, my arms and chest. The bedclothes were soaked.

"Has he been awake long?" I heard Mom ask.

Bill shook his head. "No. He was really knocked out."

Mom stood over me and dabbed at my wet skin. Directly overhead an air conditioner spewed out cool air. She frowned and threw a towel over my chest then turned to the wall and flicked a switch. Thus began a duel with one of my nurses who moved to correct the situation immediately. Back and forth they went for nearly an hour—on and off with the towel, off and on with the switch—until Dr. Guzman arrived.

"I will not have my son catching pneumonia," Mom stated flatly.

"Do anything you think best for your son regarding the temperature. I'll instruct the nurses not to interfere."

He conferred with my mother and Bill. "Robert developed an infection, but it's now under control. His leg is in good shape." He continued, "A pin, approximately fifteen inches long, has been inserted in the left thigh to hold the femur in position."

By nine-thirty that night I was in agony again. My bladder felt like it was being stretched out of shape, yet there was nothing I could do to relieve the pressure. On the doctor's authorization, two nurses appeared with a catheter. Without thinking to lubricate the tube, they struggled to force it into my penis. "Stop! *No quiero!* Take it out!" I screamed in a crazy mixture of English and Spanish. The girls ignored me, pushing the plastic tube deeper and deeper. Finally, I felt the trapped liquid starting to drain away. Again, I slept.

At three a.m. I was awakened by a fit of coughing so severe it threatened to break loose every needle and tube jutting from my body. Mom sprang from the sofa and ran for a nurse who administered another injection. As the coughing subsided, I noticed an elderly nun helping Mom back to the sofa. "*Duermate,*" she softly told Mom to sleep.

Dr. Guzman arrived early in the morning and ordered the catheter removed. After he examined me, he reported that my temperature was normal and all my signs were good. "Now it's just a matter of time," he said, "waiting until the bone knits securely." He even mentioned therapeutic exercise I could perform in bed with my upper body to circulate the blood and hasten the mending.

He had opened up the subject of time, and Mom jumped in, "But Dr. Guzman, even with exercises it'll be months before Robby can walk, won't it?"

"Yes," he answered. "The femur is the largest bone in the body and takes the longest time to heal. It will be at least three months—possible six—before he can even use crutches."

"Then he can't go back—not to prison, not to Hospital Civil. You know the condition I found him in. Without the use of his legs ... if he can't walk ... he could die!"

"I agree with you completely. I've already arranged to prolong his stay here until all danger has passed." Dr. Guzman hesitated, "I must warn you, however, that there is no guarantee."

"No guarantee? What do you mean?"

Dr. Guzman told of another prisoner he had treated, a burn victim, under court order for an indefinite stay at Sanatorio Mazatlán. One morning the doctor had gone to the hospital to treat his patient, only to find him gone—taken away by the *Federales* in the middle of the night.

That little horror story sent chills up me, and Mom looked like she was going to keel over. She swayed and grabbed for my table, her clenched knuckles as white as her face.

"What?" she breathed, her voice barely audible.

"Of course, that patient could walk," the doctor added quickly. "Your son's condition is much more serious."

I ate breakfast *con gusto*, surprising myself, downing cups of warm milk with rolls and papaya. I felt much better. The long days of fever had been vanquished. Mom sat on the couch, watching my recuperation, only stirring to ask for "*cafe negro, por favor*," when the hospital personnel passed the doorway. When I had lapped up everything in sight and lay back with satisfaction, Mom moved the tray aside. She remained standing by my bed.

"How do you feel?" she asked, and touching my face, "You're cool."

"I feel really good," I smiled. "My leg's OK—much less pain than I expected. I'm just uncomfortable under this stuff."

Mom pulled back the sheet. I saw my leg encased in a half cast, held on with elastic bandages that wound from my toes, around my leg, and around my waist.

"Right here. It's wet." I peeled back the elastic at my waist exposing red, ridged skin.

Mom brought forth talcum powder from her overnight bag and dusted the welts, then smoothed and straightened the elastic.

"Better?" she asked.

"Yes."

"Well, then . . ." She looked me over seeming to assess my condition, but left the sentence dangling. "I have to deposit the money with the cashier."

She was easy to read. Suddenly, I didn't feel so good. "I want you to thank Mike and Dinah for all they're doing back home. I know you need to go. It's OK Mom."

"I'll take the afternoon plane." When I didn't comment or change expression, she continued, "You'll be all right as long as you're here . . ." (How long will that be? I wondered.) . . . "and I need to get back to work."

She frowned slightly, "I've been trying to think of some way I can know you're safe. I can't live thinking that you might be snatched away and I wouldn't know it. Since I don't speak Spanish, I'll have Mike phone here every night to ask your condition. And if they ever say you're not here, I'll bombard the State Department and take the first plane back."

Her jaw tightened. "Don't worry. You'll never go unattended again when you're sick and helpless. Not ever!"

I believed her, and relaxed. "It'll be expensive."

"So?" She stepped quickly to the bathroom to extract cash from her bra and left the room flat-chested to leave an eight-hundred-dollar deposit in my account.

Bill arrived sick with diarrhea, appropriately called "Montezuma's Revenge" by those who contracted it in Mexico. He either sprawled on the couch, or rushed spraddle-legged to the bathroom moaning for Lomatil, while trying to coordinate escape plans.

"I'll rent a van and get Frank to drive—he's the best driver—and Paul and I can shove you out the window . . . Oh, God . . ." and again to the bathroom.

He staggered back to the couch, still talking, "The problem is the window. The panes are fixed between thick metal bars. How can we open up the window?"

"Billy?"

"Yeah? What?"

"Did you look in your pants?"

"What?" His black beard aimed at me. "What the hell are you talking about? Why should I look in my pants? I haven't shit in them and I still have my balls."

"Yesterday you told me you were going to buy some Lomatil—just in case. Did you look in your pants?"

"Oh, shit! I forgot." Bill fumbled through his pockets, placing a sundry assortment on my bedside table: cigarettes, matches, tourist card, address book, bits and pieces of paper, wadded up pesos, crumpled airline ticket, and finally, a vial—"Lomatil. I'll be damned," Bill muttered, loosening the cork and tipping out a small white pill. "I had them all the time." He popped the pill into his mouth. "OK, I'm all right now. What about the window?"

"You're all right? You just took the pill."

"So what, it's psychological. I mean it. I'm all right."

He was sitting straight up on the couch, at attention, and appeared to be in control. I began to express my thoughts. "I don't know what to do about the window. Not sure how to get out. Those bars are sturdy. I'll have to think about it."

Mom came in and handed me a receipt, folding a duplicate for her purse. "Hi, Bill. You don't look so hot. Too many margaritas last night?"

"I had a couple but I'm fine, really fine. I'll tell you all about it later."

"Uh-huh. Sure." Mom dropped the subject and focused a brilliant smile on me, "Doesn't Robby look great?"

"Yeah, a thousand percent better—just like his old self."

She looked at me. "I'm going to run out and get something for you to write on. You two can have a little time for yourselves."

"OK cousin, back to the basics," I said. "One thing we should definitely decide on right now is the time. How does two weeks sound?"

"It sounds short. Do you think you're Superman?"

"I wish. It has to happen while I'm here, and it has to happen soon." I brought Bill up to date on Dr. Guzman's story about the Feds coming for the burn patient.

"Dr. Guzman is OK. He's done a lot for me. He's honest. Wouldn't even touch Mom's money; insisted she deposit the full amount with the nuns. But I don't trust the *Federales*. Not one bit."

"O.K. Two weeks it is. But I'm not telling Barbara until the last minute."

"One more thing, and this is important." I continued. "I need you to pick up a birth certificate and tourist visa and bring them when you come back. Jesse can handle it. You'll have to slip him some money."

We began to run through plans—all the possibilities—the things that might work. We had talked for about an hour when there was a tap on the door and Mom came in carrying loose sheets of stationery and envelopes.

She turned to Bill, "I'd like you to stay another day or two. Robby will need a lot of things—he doesn't even have any clothes."

"That's fine with me, Barb," Bill agreed.

"I paid for our room through today, but you'll need more money." She handed him some dollars. "That should cover everything."

Bill stood up. "I think I'll find Jose and see if we can get together with Felix and Estela to let them know you're here.

"Good idea. Come back and let me know how they're doing. I saw a lot of homes in bad shape on my ride over here from the prison."

"I'll have dinner with you. Chateaubriand for two." He gave Mom a bear hug, "Have a safe trip, Barbara. I'll call you from the airport when I get home."

The room was quiet with Bill gone. I was suddenly exhausted. I watched Mom wipe the table with a damp towel, close the closet and bathroom doors, and straighten my sheet. She flicked the air-conditioning switch a few times, testing. There was nothing left to do.

She took my hand, looking down at me. "You're tired," she said. "Get some rest." She kissed my cheek. "See you soon."

She picked up her purse and overnight bag, then gathered the two exhibits: manila envelope with X-ray, and plastic bag with jeans. Her back to me now, I saw her straighten her shoulders and take a deep breath, standing tall. She never looked back.

Later that day Bill came back smiling and with a question.

"Do you remember the theory of mind over matter?" he asked.

"Sure…if you don't mind, it don't matter."

"That's one way to put it," he laughed. "You're going to feel much better after you hear what I have to tell you, but try to control yourself."

"Control myself. I can't even move. What are you talking about?"

"Felix is bringing Estela here on Saturday."

"Yahoo cousin!" I yelled. "You made my day."

"Now the really good news. He invited me to the restaurant and we're going to surprise Lupe."

"No wonder you've had that smirk on your face since you got here. And I thought it was for me. You lucky dog." We high fived as he left, smiles on both our faces.

The next morning Dr. Arriaga appeared. The surgeon had played it scarce since the operation, leaving the daily drop-ins to Dr. Guzman. Seeing him now made me uncomfortable. He was totally lacking in bedside manner.

"You're wasting valuable bed space," he told me following a cursory examination. "Our job is basically finished. You need rest, but you can get that any place."

I swallowed hard. "But I'm still weak. I can't do anything for myself."

The doctor ran a palm across his graying hairline. "What I'm saying is, soon we will take your stitches out—then you will no longer require medically trained personnel to assist you."

"I can't even go to the bathroom by myself. And what about complications? I'm sure you're aware of the disease and infection I'll be exposed to if I'm sent back to the prison in my condition."

"All real danger is passed. You have nothing to fear."

That's what you think, doctor, I thought. I decided to change my approach.

"I spoke with my attorney yesterday," I said. "It looks like my release will be secured any time. He's working with the authorities to have me transferred directly to a hospital in California."

Dr. Arriaga registered some surprise and left without further threats to have me relocated; but without saying that I'd be allowed to remain at Sanatorio Mazatlán.

The good came the next day. It was Saturday and my visitors arrived right after lunch. My bed was facing the entrance and when my door opened, four visitors entered. Estela, Blanca, a little girl, and Felix with a big grin on his face.

"Ay Roberto, you're looking better than I thought you would," said Felix. "They taking good care of you?"

"Be happy you didn't see me a few days ago. I'm coming back to life. Come on over and give me an *abrazo*," I motioned for all of them and got three hugs and a handshake from the little girl who offered me some *coricos*.

"This is Blanca's niece, Ramoncita. She wanted to bring you some *coricos* made by her grandmother. They were like shortbread cookies in the shape of a skinny doughnut with a hole in the middle.

"*Gracias*," I said, putting one in my mouth. "Mmm *deliciosa*." Ramoncita was smiling.

'She'll bring you more next time if you like these." said Blanca. She sells them on the street every weekend."

"I would love that, and be sure to tell grandma how much I like them."

"We're going to pass some of these out to the nurses and patients and let you two have some time alone." said Felix.

They walked out and closed the door behind them. Estela had seemed quiet and shy when they entered but she didn't waste any time coming straight to my side and giving me a kiss that dreams are made of.

"Roberto, I missed you so much. You were so close I could feel you, but I couldn't see you.

"Now you can do both. I'd break my leg anytime to be with you."

I could feel the connection as our hands closed together. A warmth moved through my whole body. I gave her a quick description of what I had gone through since we were picked up by the Feds outside the disco…skipping the depressing parts.

"I didn't know what happened to you and when we tried to find out, they would tell us nothing. Felix finally got a message to me from Jose. Inside, I felt you…here." placing her hand on her heart.

"I sent you messages through my mind, hoping you would get them."

"I did. Now I can receive them in person. Much better." she said smiling.

Felix returned with Blanca and Ramoncita, recounting their success in passing out *coricos*.

"Everybody loved them," Felix said. "Her bag is almost empty."

"I hope you can come back again," I told Ramoncita.

"*Si señor,*" she smiled.

Felix had the girls go outside so we could talk alone.

"I want you to know, anything you need *mano*, anything, I'm here for you," Felix offered.

"*Gracias, amigo.* I know I can count on you and I may need your help when we decide what to do. One thing you can count on; I'm not going back to that jungle."

"I know. Bill had a good talk to me before he left. Just remember, I can stop by anytime. El Marinero's only ten minutes away."

"Good to know. For now, it's safer to stay out of sight until Bill gets back. I don't want the guards to get to know you in case we want the element of surprise. Estela will visit me on weekends, and Gretchen stops by in the mornings to check on me. I'll get word to you."

We shook on it and Felix left. I knew I would be seeing him again.

# 12

## Stretcher Plan

O n Sunday, Jose stopped by. He had been thinking of ways to help me and mentioned that a good friend of his was captain of a large fishing boat in Mazatlán. All our previous escape thinking had been geared to land travel and air, but the open sea offered new possibilities. The Gulf of California was a relatively calm body of water; much easier to navigate than the often—choppy Pacific that lay on the other side of the Baja peninsula—and we wouldn't encounter roadblocks along the way.

I told him to ask his friend if he might be willing to take me up the Gulf as far as San Felipe. It was often full of American tourists and not too far from the US. With Bill's help I could probably arrange to have a camper or van waiting to carry me northward across the border and home. Jose said he would make inquiries and report back.

How I was going to leave Mazatlán was secondary to getting out of the hospital safely. That needed to be our first focal point. I looked at the window with the bars behind me. With the front door closed at night and a sleeping guard on his chair in front of the door, I just needed to find a way to get out the window. I thought about it every night.

The guards at my door worked twelve-hour shifts, starting at eight in the morning. They were replaced every three days. Guards would often to mingle with visitors and hospital personnel. My new night guard, Pepe, was a Don Juan of sorts—young, hip, and cool. His form-fitting slacks and neat blue shirt designed to catch the eyes of the ladies did just that as he posed and strutted in macho style outside my room. With the end of visiting hours nearing and a slowdown in female foot traffic, he deserted his post to relax on the sofa across from my bed. His first night on duty, he came in around eight-thirty, and asked if I wanted to smoke a joint with him. I declined, saying I was already stoned from the medication they were pumping into me.

Later that evening Pepe left to greet several nurses who had just come on duty. When I saw him again, he was in the company of an older man, also a city policeman, named Gilberto. He worked night patrol in the neighborhood and had missed dinner. "Could I interest both of you in some chicken?" he asked in Spanish. Pepe and I accepted and he was out the door heading for the nearby Pollos Locos. What followed was like an old-fashioned picnic, the three of us laughing and talking as though we were longtime friends, not watchmen and prisoner.

Pepe and Gilberto came to my room the following night. Pepe smoked marijuana openly and talked of his adventures with the ladies—and his troubles. He was married, living with his wife, and was about to become a father. But it was not his wife who was pregnant. Another girl carried his child. She had gone to the Chief of Police with her news and Pepe was ordered to support her.

Gilberto mentioned having trouble surviving on his earnings as a policeman. "This is no life for a man of my years," he said in a low voice. "I'm getting old. And fifty pesos does not buy much."

Pepe talked of easier money, shaking down tourists he'd find on the streets or on the beach at night. "It's not difficult. Mention marijuana and jail in the same breath and I'm holding a ten-dollar bill. That's more than what I make in an entire day."

I talked of America and the fresh start they could find there. And the riches. "My father owns a construction company near Los Angeles," I said. "You could live very comfortably on the big money you'd make every week."

Without hesitating, Pepe said, "For a good salary and the right setup, I'd be tempted to leave and start over again."

Gilberto was not as keen to leave, but money definitely interested him. It was only natural the subject of my getting home should come up. I stopped short of using the word--escape. I approached the subject jokingly. "You guys have a home to go to every night. Not me. If I could get out of this mess, I'd be glad to show you my town and help you get a good paying job."

Pepe and Gilberto laughed politely then talked again of their need for money. But that's as much as they'd say. I decided not to press too hard, too soon.

Gretchen stopped by almost every day on her way to CPM. There wasn't a guard who didn't like her. She was young, attractive, and friendly. More than anyone else, she helped break the ice with my newly assigned guards. A few minutes of conversation with Gretchen and they seemed more *simpático* toward their bedridden prisoner.

I was telling Gretchen of my last session with Pepe and Gilberto when I noticed Gilberto standing in the corridor. "What's he doing here now?" I wondered aloud. "Something funny's going on." Gretchen left, and minute later he was at my side inquiring about my health. From the expression on his face, he had more than that on his mind. Gilberto pulled a chair close to my bed.

"I was thinking about our talk last night," he said in low tones. "Possibly we can help each other."

"I'm sure we can," I said.

"Good," he smiled. He looked over his left shoulder toward the door before going on. "You can't leave this building without documents showing the official police stamp. I can arrange to get them for you."

"The official documents will be accepted by the hospital staff without question. It's not unusual. They know that a patient who is a Federal prisoner may be transferred at any time, regardless of his condition."

"The hospital might accept them, but what about the guard on duty?"

"The only way we can get this man to leave his post for any length of time is to send him out to bring in another prisoner patient. This requires a phone call using key phrases that automatically tell him the call is originating from police headquarters. If the code words are missing, he won't respond."

"How do you do that?"

"Pepe's working on it. His uncle was in charge of communications and knows all the codes."

I accepted Gilberto's statement without committing myself. I didn't really know the man or feel I could trust him. Not yet.

It was clear from the start that three people—Gilberto, Bill and I—couldn't pull off the escape by ourselves. We needed two others, Mexicans, to pose as *Federales* and carry the stretcher to the getaway vehicle.

As much as I wanted to work with Jose, I decided against it. His face was too familiar among hospital personnel and had earlier been interrogated by the Feds.

I thought of my friend, Felix. Bill and I had met him on our first trip to Mazatlán and he happily showed us the secrets of the town that only a local would know. Whether it was a restaurant hideaway with great food and music, a secret beach, or historical mountain villages—Felix was happy to be our unofficial guide. The temptation to rule out my young friend was great, but I kept remembering his repeated offers to help. "If you ever need me," he had said, "call at any time. My country owes you."

Gretchen sent word to Felix that I wanted to see him. When I explained my plan, he jumped at the chance to help, even before I could ask. It turned out that Felix had a good friend, Armando, who worked as a waiter in one of the local hotels. Armando owned a van. He was planning on driving south to Tepic to visit his mother as soon as he could save enough money. For three thousand pesos, Armando agreed to provide his services as well as the transportation. Gilberto and Pepe came in for slightly more: six thousand each to be paid when I was safely inside the van. My crew was working at cut-rate prices. I asked Felix to call Bill and tell him to bring the money and the papers I had asked him to get.

The phone at the reception desk rang every night at approximately seven pm. The calls were long distance—from Los Angeles—and the voice on the other end always belonged to Mike, my stepfather. In fluent Spanish, he would ask, "What is Robert Miller's condition tonight? Does he have any message for his mother?" The routine never varied since the purpose of the calls was to make sure I was still a patient in the hospital.

Bill had not been idle since his last visit. He had been plotting an escape route, recruiting personnel, and obtaining a getaway van. When he told me that three of my friends—Jerry, Frank, and Paul—had volunteered to drive, I was speechless. These friends were not blood relatives like Bill, yet they were willing to jeopardize their freedom and safety to help me.

"I've checked out all possible routes on the map and this one seems the shortest way out of Mexico," Bill said, marking a line through Mazatlán and Durango up to the Texas border.

"I know a shorter one, and it's much faster," I smiled.

"Impossible. We've checked mileage and time charts for the last week."

"All right, Cousin, now that you're here in person I can clue you in. All of my talk about driving north was for the benefit of Gilberto—in case he isn't so trustworthy after he's been paid. And besides, those roads have Federal checkpoints in different locations, and near the end of your route is the biggest checkpoint in Mexico. It never closes."

"That's what we were afraid of."

"That's why I've decided to fly over them."

"Top banana?" he asked.

"You guessed it. All the way, and that's why I need that tourist visa. You brought it, right?

"Jesse took care of both the birth certificate and the visa. Anything you need, he's ready to help."

I explained the "Stretcher Plan" to Bill and asked him to make sure Felix and Armando were completely together. He would personally supervise the trial run to the airport and pick up the tickets for himself and the injured American tourist.

When Bill came to the hospital that evening, I introduced him to our co-conspirator, Gilberto. Bill and Gilberto walked to a nearby bar where Pepe was waiting. Details were finalized and the escape was set for two p.m. on Thursday.

On Thursday morning Felix and Armando made another trial run to the airport to double check the elapsed time. Bill picked up the tickets for the flight—Mazatlán to Tucson to Los Angeles—set to depart at four o'clock. It was the same flight Mom had taken almost three weeks earlier. This time, she had arranged for an ambulance to meet the flight and her personal physician was standing by, having reserved a hospital room in my name.

Timing was all important. The guard would be called to the phone at exactly two o'clock. Pepe would give him the code, plus orders to go to the emergency medical center across town where he was to pick up an injured prisoner for admittance to Sanatorio Mazatlán. Elapsed time for this wild goose chase, including travel to the medical center, confusion over the mythical prisoner and return to the hospital, was estimated at just under two hours. There was no telling how long it would take him to discover my disappearance, once he returned. By then I would be in the air, safe and free.

Gilberto visited me late that morning to hand over the official looking papers for Felix and Armando to show at the front desk. He assured me everything was in place. I gave the papers to Bill when he stopped by to tell me all was good on his end.

Esperanza brought the lunch tray just past noon and I barely touched it. My stomach churned. If Esperanza noticed a change in my composure, she didn't say anything. Even the picked-over plate was removed without comment. I couldn't help wonder if she suspected what was about to happen.

By one forty-five p.m. I was ticking off everyone's assignments in my head. Felix and Armando, I told myself, are with Pepe driving to a telephone. Felix would be with Pepe to make sure he made the call, then he and Armando would arrive to pick me up. I sat up tall in bed to look out the window; I could see Gilberto across the street. Bill was at the airport, undoubtedly checking his watch and wishing he had a different bloodline.

I took a deep breath, settled back in bed, and began counting the minutes.

At two on the dot, I heard the desk phone ringing. A nun summoned my guard and he left his post. One minute passed, then five, then ten. Where were Felix and Armando?

Suddenly, my door opened wide. Felix rushed in—alone and empty-handed. "Where's the stretcher?" I asked. "And Armando?"

His face was wet with perspiration. "In the van," he answered, uneasily.

"Well, go get them—we've got to move. We're wasting time."

"Something's wrong," he said. "The guard hasn't left yet."

"What do you mean he hasn't left?"

"He went to the front and looked around and came back. I think he knows something."

"Where is he?"

Felix didn't respond. He hurried into the bathroom and closed the door. Then the guard came in looking around and asked a strange question, "Feel like a game of cards?"

"Not right now, maybe later," I said. "I'm waiting for a lady friend."

Instead of going back outside, the guard went for the bathroom and opened the door. When he saw Felix, he pulled out his gun.

No one said a word as Felix was taken from the bathroom and brought to my side with a gun pointed at him. "Do you know this man?" the guard asked in Spanish.

God, don't let me blow this!

I cleared my throat and, half smiling, answered, "He's a friend of mine."

"Why was he hiding?"

A good question.

"I was waiting for Gretchen," Felix answered. "I was going to surprise her."

The guard's eyes narrowed. "Who is Gretchen?"

"She's my girlfriend," I said. "She comes every day. You must have seen her."

Felix nodded. "We play jokes on each other all the time. I was going to jump out and scare her."

The guard's icy expression began melting. He looked at me. "Is this the lady friend you are waiting for?"

I nodded in the affirmative.

"She's blond and beautiful," Felix offered.

A sly grin broke on the policeman's face.

Then he started laughing. "I'll be outside—waiting for this Gretchen to arrive." He went out and Felix closed the door behind him.

"I'm sorry," Felix whispered. "I choked."

"You covered up fine," I said.

"What now?"

"Go see Bill at the airport. Tell him to get on the plane. Something went wrong and I want him safe so we can finish this later. The stretcher plan's dead. You'd better stay away until we know what's going on. I'll send word to you with Jose or Estela.

The next day Jose opened the door to the room. As I waved him inside, he shot an ugly look toward my guard, then closed the door.

"¡*Cabrón*!" he snarled. "When did they start getting so tough around here?"

"What happened?"

"Patted me up and down. In front of Mother Superior."

I motioned for Jose to sit. "That's sure going to make things a lot harder."

"Why?"

"They're on to me. This guard's been hovering all morning, looking in every few minutes. It's not because he's worried about my health, that's for sure."

Quickly, I told Jose about the stretcher plan and the fiasco with Felix and the guard.

He walked to the window and stood with his back to me. He was silent for a time before he asked, "Why didn't you tell me about your plan?"

"You were the first person I thought of," I said. "But they know you're my friend."

"I'm not ashamed of that."

"I couldn't risk involving you. You have family and they know where to find you."

Jose snickered. "I make that decision, not you." Do you want to get out of here?"

"You know I do—but everything must be right. I don't want to get caught and sent back to the prison."

Jose turned from the window to face me. "Then let me help you."

"I'm open for ideas. Bill and I zeroed out."

"Where is your cousin now?"

"I sent him back on the plane. I still don't know what happened, or who's safe."

I was quiet for a moment. "You have a plan?" I asked.

"I'm thinking," he answered.

"There's no way to get me through the halls and out of this place. You just saw how tight security is now.

"What about night?"

"You still have the guard sitting directly in front of my door."

Jose cut me off with a wave then walked back to the window to run his fingers along the metal bars.

"Watch it," I cautioned him. "The guard might look in again."

Jose drew his hand away. Then, almost casually, he stated, "I think I have a way."

"Tell me," I said. I waited, but he continued to study the construction of the grill. "Is it the window? Is that your way?"

"It wouldn't be difficult."

"Too noisy. Put a file to one of those bars and you'd have a gun in your back."

"No files, no noise. It would be very quiet," he assured me.

"How?"

"Acid… I have someone who can run some tests to see if it would work."

"Do it! There's also a night patrol on the streets and we need to know his schedule."

Jose left, determined to help me. I remembered the story about his younger days when he was a bodyguard for two brothers who were big marijuana suppliers before they were arrested at the behest of the US government. Maybe he missed the old days and wanted some excitement, but I felt there was more to it. We were friends. He knew the hell I'd gone through for something I wasn't involved in, and wanted to right the wrong.

On Saturday, the nuns were making their rounds, offering blessings and prayers. Rafa, my new guard, told me that a young lady was waiting at the front desk. I thought of Gretchen at once, although it was not like her to be so formal. "Bring her in," I told him. I raised my bed and waited.

There was something special about Estela. She moved towards me with her graceful walk as a smile radiated from her face that captivated me. She was attractive, but it was that special something that came from within that touched me the most. Beside my bed, her eyes told me all I needed to know. Estela wasn't holding back today.

"Let me be next to you" she said as I made room for the tight fit. We embraced and became lost in a long kiss.

"Hold me," she said. "I just want to feel you."

We didn't talk. The energy between us was enough. Just as I felt I couldn't hold back any more, the guard opened the door and broke the spell.

"How about some privacy?" I told him. "You know I can't go anywhere. Give us some time alone."

The guard looked at us both, turned around and walked out without closing the door. Estela remained sitting on the bed.

"How have you been, Roberto?" she asked me.

'A lot has happened, but I'm doing better now. How's school and the children?

"They certainly keep me busy. I really enjoy helping them learn and opening their inquisitive minds. Some of the questions they ask are so beyond their age, while others make me want to fall over laughing." she smiled.

"Makes me think of Ramoncita and her *coricos*. "What a delicious surprise."

"You enjoyed them, and that made her happy... Do you know about the "Dia de la Virgen de Guadalupe?"

"I've seen her image all over Mexico. Chuy set up an altar with candles in the prison. She must be very special."

"She is the patron saint of Mexico and I will tell you a brief version of the story."

"Juan Diego, an indigenous Indian was walking in the Hills of Tepeyac when he was stopped by the appearance of the Virgen, a young woman with black hair and brown skin. She told Juan Diego to go to the Bishop and have him build a church on the Hill of Tepeyac. Juan Diego went to the Bishop and told him the story of how the Virgen had sent him to tell the Bishop to build a church. The Bishop didn't believe him and Juan Diego left, saddened. On

December 12, the Virgen appeared again and instructed Juan Diego to go to the top of the Hill of Tepeyac and collect flowers to bring to the Bishop. Juan Diego felt compelled to go, even though he knew flowers did not grow on that barren hill, especially in December. When he reached the top, he couldn't believe his eyes--beautiful and colorful flowers he had never seen before were miraculously growing everywhere. Juan Diego put some flowers in his cloak and carried them to the Bishop. When the flowers were removed, the image of the Virgen remained on the cloak. Both the Bishop and Juan Diego were now believers. The *Basilica de La Virgen de Guadalupe* was soon built on the Hill of Tepeyac and there are celebrations all over Mexico on December 12th."

"Thank you for the history lesson."

"You're welcome. The reason I want you to know this story is because December 12th is almost here. Now you will know the history as the parade passes by in the evening. You can see it from your window. Ramoncita and her grandmother will be nearby passing out *buñuelos* that you will not be able to resist."

"I'll be dreaming about them, along with you." I said.

Suddenly I heard a familiar clicking sound at the door. Jefe, and his stocky sidekick, Gordo entered my room. Estela froze, and my heart was pounding rapidly.

He sneered at me as I focused on the scar on his left cheek.

"Eh Gringo, I hear you've been getting ideas. Making trouble," Jefe said. Gordo was at the door waiting for instructions.

"What trouble, I can't even move. You have nothing to worry about."

He pulled Estela off the bed, lifted the blanket, and pounded his knuckles on my cast.

"You are in federal custody, my custody. I hear that you want to leave."

"Keep your hands off of him!" Estela insisted, as she picked up the blanket and put it back over me. "He doesn't belong here and you know who the real *mafiosas* are."

Jefe stopped and glared at her.

"Be very careful. Our government wants Americans, but if you like I can make an exception for you."

'You just try it," she said firmly, "I know people too. What you're doing is wrong and you know it?"

"I just follow orders," he hesitated, looking around the room. He held his eyes on Estela. "Next time I come back, he will be leaving with me." He nodded to Gordo, and they were off.

# 13

## *Wheels*

Huge reflective discs hovered overhead as Dr. Arriaga worked with snippers and tweezers pulling pieces of fine knotted wire from my leg. The cast had been removed. The stitches were nearly gone. Soon a new cast would be applied and I would return to my room.

"You have a visitor this morning," the doctor informed me. "The warden is here to check on your progress."

I had an uncomfortable feeling he had more than that in mind.

The reigning monarch of the prison was seated comfortably on my sofa, reading a newspaper, when my gurney, guided by a duo of attendants, reached the door.

Dr. Arriaga entered first. "Good afternoon," he said in Spanish.

The two men exchanged a few words while I was lifted onto clean sheets. Then their attention focused on me.

The warden was full of questions about my health.

I told him I felt pain with every movement, from the pin tearing into my muscles. "It's not healing properly."

The doctor shook his head, said a few words, and left.

"What do you think of returning to *Correccionales*?" the warden asked.

Did I detect concern in his voice—or was it only wishful thinking?

"My attorney is having me transferred directly from here to a hospital near home. The deal is almost set. I would like to stay in the hospital until then."

"When?"

"I should be home for Christmas. I was hoping to stay here until then so I could have the best medical care in case of complications."

The warden nodded. "Two, three weeks then?"

"At the most," I stated. "My attorney tells me I'm to be found not guilty. He's already spoken with the judge."

"My experience tells me these things don't always happen as planned," the warden commented. "Or as quickly."

"I would appreciate it if you'd let me stay here. I can't even get out of bed by myself. And you know how difficult it would be for me back in the prison."

"Well," the warden said, "we'll see what happens."

The warden smiled and offered his hand. "Perhaps we should talk another time before a decision is made."

"Yes, we should," I said, thinking that would be the time to slip him a little *mordida*. Better have some cash on hand.

Then he excused himself. Outside the room he paused momentarily and I overheard him ask my guard, "How is the prisoner behaving?"

What could the man say? Since my session with the guards and Felix, I lived every moment as though I were in a glass bubble. I had been friendly, not only with nurses and doctors, but with my guards as well. Only Gretchen had visited me. I received no messages. Even the customary night calls from home were answered routinely by the front desk. If the authorities had been suspicious, their minds could rest easier now.

The next morning brought a surprise that would change everything. Esperanza came in followed by another nurse, Socorro, who was pushing a wheelchair.

"Is that for me?" my eyes widening.

"What do you think?"

"I love it, but I think we have a problem," I told her. "I can't bend my leg."

She held up an index finger and her assistant returned with a flat board.

"I'll show you," she said. She helped me into the wheelchair with my good leg while Socorro held the cast. They raised the left foot-rest until it was even with the seat and placed the board across the top. A pillow was added and my cast lifted and placed on top of it.

"Now what do you think?" she asked.

I never knew sitting in a chair could be such a thrill. I felt like a little kid with his first bike. I could move with my feet off the ground. I was mobile.

I smiled, impishly, then answered with total understatement, "I like it."

"Good," Esperanza sighed. "You will use it every morning while I change your bed."

"Hey, who's supposed to benefit from this thing, you or me?"

"Both," she winked.

The wheelchair literally opened doors for me. I found myself out in the corridor talking with my guard, greeting the nurses, and meeting some of the patients. There was an open-air courtyard I could wheel into and enjoy colorful flowers under the sun and lovely blue sky.

Back in my room another nurse had helped me get from my wheelchair to my bed. I was getting the hang of it and decided to practice doing it by myself. I would lower the bed then stand on my good leg with bent knee into the seat as I reached out to slowly lower the cast from the bed. I could feel the pin inside my bone wiggling, and I was in pain. Practice makes perfect, I thought. For now, I would ask for help, especially getting back onto the bed.

That evening I was able to hear the sounds of home. When Mike asked the receptionist for messages, he was asked to wait to while a nurse came for me. I was wheeled to the desk and surprised Mike. Soon my mother was on the phone, laughing, crying, asking questions. The answers weren't always forthcoming. I wanted to talk openly, but had to be careful what I said over the phone, especially with a guard nearby. For the moment, however, knowing I had a direct line to my family was enough to satisfy me.

Only Dr. Arriaga tarnished the glow I felt that evening. "Where do you think you are going?" he asked. I was wheeling from the desk back to my room.

His stern voice startled me. "Nowhere," I answered.

"Who gave you permission to be here?"

I told him the wheelchair was part of my therapy.

"You are still a prisoner," he said coldly. "Do not leave your room."

I laughed. "How can I escape in a wheelchair? And like this?" I pointed to my newly plastered leg. It looked like a battering ram with toes.

Dr. Arriaga was not about to tell me twice. He called the nurse. I found myself shoved quickly toward the white walls of my room. Give it a few days, I told myself.

I tried not to let the doctor's attitude bother me. Compared to the warden, he didn't wield any clout—and I had a feeling the warden would at least see me again before he made a move. My gut feeling could not suppress fact that I was still at risk. With Jefe gleefully in charge, the fear still persisted that any night I might be taken away. Gretchen didn't ease my mind any when she told me that Julio and the others who had shared my room at the Hospital Civil were now back at CPM, their recoveries far from complete. I was the only casualty of the storm, yet to return.

For the next couple of days as Esperanza changed my sheets, I was able to cruise around the hospital. I met many of the nurses and patients as I wheeled by, some even inviting me into their rooms.

Each day I became more familiar with hospital routine. I learned the schedules of key personnel. I discovered the facility's peak and slow periods. Morning and early evening were busy. Always. Early afternoon and late evening were slow. I was particularly impressed with the period from 1:00 to 3:00 p.m. Except for the inside guard and two nurses, the corridors were deserted. Without fail, the entire staff, including the nuns, disappeared for lunch while many patients napped.

Before I knew it, December 12 had arrived, and with it an evening visit from Estela and Blanca. I showed off my new wheelchair and they were excited enough to ask the Mother Superior for permission to wheel me near the entrance to watch the parade. Ramoncita came in with her basket and was handing the guard a *buñuelo* (cinnamon sugar pastry) as I was being wheeled out of my room. He followed us out and we all enjoyed the parade together. I held my *buñuelo* with one hand, while feeling Estela's warmth in the other. The parade was much grander than I had expected. Various groups of musicians passed by with their instruments, while others carried placards with images of the Virgen de Guadalupe. Young and old, wearing costumes and masks, danced jubilantly to the music as the procession moved forward. I had a feeling something good was about to happen.

The days at the hospital became more eventful. An American passenger from one of the cruise ships from Long Beach, had been admitted with chest pains. The man was in his early seventies and spoke no Spanish. Neither did his wife. She complained about the room—the air conditioning did not function—and demanded a change. He couldn't read the menu and refused to eat certain items substituted for those he thought he ordered. I was brought in to interpret. The switch in rooms was easily accomplished. Once the gentleman realized he was on a special diet, his appetite improved.

My reputation as a linguist quickly spread. I didn't realize how far until Mother Superior came to see me. Previously, we had nodded on occasion in the corridor. Now she wanted me to tutor her in English. The Reverend Mother admitted having formal instruction years before, but her teacher, she said, had talked too fast.

She laughed as she told me, "The few words I did learn, are of no use to me here."

She returned to my room the following morning, armed with a tape recorder. I drew up a long list of conversational phrases she could use with visiting Americans: What is your name? Where does it hurt? What would you like to eat? And so on. We arranged to meet once a day. I enjoyed teaching her and watching her expression when she mastered an assignment.

I received a letter from Jon urging me to deposit fifteen thousand dollars in a Mexican bank by January 3rd. "Mel is ready to move, but the money must be in the bank or the deal will fall through." The only bright spot was his end remark that the judge was on vacation for the full month of December.

I started to read Jon's note to my mother when she called that evening.

"I just talked with him on the phone and that fifteen thousand-dollar figure hit me hard. All the time I thought it was ten thousand. How did it get up to fifteen?" she asked.

"Ten thousand was for the escrow account to put us on top of the list. Gary ended up paying sixteen thousand."

"Maybe I didn't want to think any higher than ten, so it became fixed in my mind." She paused, then murmured as if to herself, "Maybe I'm going nuts."

"Hey, Mom. Take it easy."

"OK." Her voice was strong again. "I'll think about going nuts tomorrow. Right now, I'll bring you up-to-date on our money situation. Mike and I are getting $7000 on our house; and I have two promises: one for $10,000, and one for payment of all your legal fees. If either one comes through, we can make it."

"Is there a problem with the promises?"

"Isn't there always?"

I decided to find a way out that would not require Mom mortgaging her house. Although I believed Jon was sincere and Mel had been successful with Gary, the only way I felt completely confident was to have the key to freedom in my own hands. Having the wheelchair had changed everything especially since it was common for me to be out of my room making my rounds, translating, or greeting fellow patients for hours at a time. The guards had changed constantly and seemed less interested in my movements. Of course, they were always stationed in that chair outside my door. I had noticed a number of times that a door in the corridor at the back of the hospital where trash was taken out was left open. It led to another door that opened to the outside. A plan came to mind and I began to write a letter:

*Dear Mom,*

*I'm not sure how the money is coming or if you'll ever collect enough for the deposit. But maybe, just maybe, we won't need it.*

*Sitting at the back door today I realized how many times I could have escaped if only a car was waiting for me. Now with the holidays coming, it should be even easier. Escaping from the hospital is no good if I'm captured at a roadblock and sent back to prison. I'm formulating a plan that will take me home safely and quickly. I've been told by reliable sources that there are no roadblocks on Christmas Eve and New Year's Eve, in most of Mexico. Estela's family is visiting her grandmother in Nayarit for Christmas and I will find out if the coast was clear. If you can handle the logistics and necessary reservations, I can fly direct from Guadalajara to the US—anywhere as long as it's the first flight out on New Year's Day. I choose Guadalajara in the south because they'll probably be looking for me to head north to the border. It's a large city and has the largest number of Americans living in Mexico—so I'll fit right in. If Bill wants to do it and has a together crew, I'm ready. But please, let it be his decision, and only if he truly wants to.*

When Gretchen took the letter that afternoon, I felt a sense of achievement. Just knowing it was on its way home sent visions dancing before my eyes. I had barely settled back when a gray-haired man, a complete stranger, poked his head into the room.

"Robert Miller?" he asked, squinting through thick glasses.

I nodded and he cautiously stepped inside. His eyes darted across the ceiling to the window, around the walls and along the baseboard. He crossed to the sofa and ran his fingers down the seams and into the crevices. Then he was on his hands and knees looking under the bed.

Finally, he stood, and putting his hands to his ears, whispered in Spanish," Is the room bugged?"

He was like a character in a silent movie. I wanted to laugh but thought better of it. "I don't think so," I replied.

The man moved very close and introduced himself as one of the top officials in the state government. "A friend who works for the courthouse in Beverly Hills," he said softly, "asked me to step in and help with your case."

I frowned.

"Don't be concerned, please. There are reports of a new District Attorney. And a new judge. You will be taken care of." He smiled nervously, then backed toward the door. "I'll return when I know more."

I didn't know whether to take him seriously or send for the butterfly net.

Mom didn't call that evening or the next. She had mentioned the telephone bill skyrocketing. "We've got to cut down some-place," she had said. When five nights passed without word, I began fidgeting. I had to know if she'd received my letter and their reaction to it.

I mistakenly thought it was her when I was helped into my wheelchair for a phone call. Jon was on the line, calling to tell me that soon he would be heading to Mexico City to finalize arrangements with Mel for my release. He wanted to confirm that the money would be in the bank by the third.

"My mother's trying to raise it now," I said truthfully. "If she's successful, it'll be in the bank in time."

There was a slight pause. "You don't sound too sure."

"She's working on it."

"I'd like to help," he said. 'If you're a little short, don't worry. I'll put in whatever you need."

Jon had been a good friend. He had already spent a great deal of his own money flying back and forth to Mazatlán and Mexico City on my behalf. His only reward would be my freedom. I was deeply touched by the offer and I told him so.

The emotion in my voice flustered him and he tried to change the mood.

"Getting you home is more important than a few bucks," he said, promising to call back before the deadline.

Mom phoned nearly a week after my letter had been mailed. She was down. The contributors were hedging, she said. The money so generously pledged in October and November was not coming through.

"What do they say? What excuse do they give?"

"They give me a bunch of bullshit. They say they'll get the money out of the bank and call me back, and they never call back. And so, I call—and call and call—and all I hear are phones ringing and no one picking up."

I knew Mom had pursued every avenue trying to raise the money. She knew what she was doing; she'd been at it long enough. "Mel is our best shot with the legal route" I told her. "And probably our last one. Do you think somebody's trying to tell us something?"

She didn't hesitate in answering. "I received your letter," she said.

"Yes."

"I'm with you. I think it's the way to go."

"Thank God!" And Billy?"

"He's ready. We're all together in this." She paused, then asked, "Can we talk?"

"We have to. There isn't much time."

"We need more details."

"I'll get them off to you tomorrow. At least I have something to shoot for now."

"We all do, Robby. It's going to be fine."

"I know it," I said.

Late that night, when the corridors were quiet, I wrote an outline of the escape as I envisioned it. Upon arriving in Mazatlán, they would rent a car ... it would be parked at the hospital's rear entrance at a pre-determined time on New Year's Eve ... After leaving by the rear door we would drive south to Guadalajara and then board a plane home in the early morning. "I'll leave the reservations and details to Mom," I wrote, "And don't forget to bring me some casual dress clothes."

If the Reverend Mother noticed a change in my behavior, she didn't comment. My concentration was nil. Gretchen was later than usual and I was anxious to get the letter mailed. With one ear I listened to the Mother Superior repeating her phrases. With the other I strained to hear Gretchen's footsteps in the hall. My letter to Bill still sat on my nightstand.

When she finally appeared, breathless and apologetic, my pupil was gone. Gretchen had been shopping for a present for Esperanza. I had given her money and she had canvassed all the local shops to find the right thing. "I hope you like it," she said, holding up a shimmering chain necklace with a cross. I nodded my approval.

"One more favor," I reached for the letter. "This has to get out today."

"No problem," she smiled and started to leave.

"Thanks for all your help."

Gretchen looked at me, her eyes at once sympathetic and tender. She nodded slowly. Then she hurried away. Just in time I found out a little later.

Esperanza brought my dinner and set it on the tray above my bed. As I sat up, the door opened and Jefe stood facing me with his two cohorts.

"Your vacation is over, Gringo!"

"What are you talking about. I'm being transferred back home"

"The only home you're being transferred to, is prison. The warden is waiting for you."

Esperanza said nothing and left hurriedly.

Was this a shakedown, I wondered? Did he want money?

Jefe walked to the bed and ripped off the blanket and the sheet. Mother Superior marched in with Esperanza right behind her.

"Stop this immediately! What do you think you are doing?"

Jefe stared at her menacingly, but she did not budge.

"Don't get in my way," he said.

"Where are your papers?

"Papers? I don't need no papers for a Gringo."

"Yes, you do! You may get away with your atrocities out there, but in here, I am in charge."

Jefe stared at her in anger. She held her ground. Esperanza made the sign of the cross. Jefe turned to give me an evil look.

"I'll be back with the papers," and turned to Mother Superior. "If God don't mind."

"*Vámonos*," he ordered, as the three of them stomped out.

I thanked Mother Superior and she assured me that I would be safe as long as I was in the care of her hospital. She would not allow any monkey business under her watch.

Christmas was nearing and Estela came by to see me before her trip with the family to visit her grandmother in Nayarit. It was early evening and we could hear the voices of children caroling outside my window. She sat on the bed next to me and we listened to some of my favorite Christmas songs, in Spanish. Though far away from home, I felt the spirit as never before. I just knew things were going to work out. I let her know about my plans to escape and asked her to tell Felix whether the roadblocks were open or closed on her trip. I explained that it would be better if she did not come back to visit. I would see her again when I was a free man. I didn't want my escape to cause problems for any of the people that I cared about.

"I will pray to the Virgen. She will protect you. *Vaya con Dios, Roberto.*" And then she kissed me.

I don't really know how to compare kisses with Estela because they were all so profound, but I would swear this one was just a little longer and deeper than the others that had preceded it. My head was spinning when she left, and I didn't have a care in the world.

On Christmas Eve, I was fortunate to have the company of Felix and Gretchen. Away from home and separated from our families, we would celebrate together. Felix was from the state of Tabasco, in southern Mexico. He had told me stories of his mother's fabulous *mole* which she cooked only on special occasions and was copied by many, but never duplicated. It contained chocolate, peanuts, chile, raisins, and seventeen secret spices. The sauce would cook for hours over many days before being ready to be eaten with roasted chicken. She had sent some sauce to his uncle in Mazatlán for Christmas and now Felix was sharing the chicken mole, tamales, and a special Christmas drink with a kick to it, called *ponche*, with the two of us. This was unlike any Christmas I had ever known.

The *ponche* took effect and we were laughing at a joke from Felix when the nurse came in to tell me that my mother was on the line. I wheeled myself to the phone at the front desk.

Mom began with a "Merry Christmas."

"*Feliz Navidad,*" I replied.

"How are you doing?" she asked.

"Fantastic, we're celebrating." I told her.

"We?"

"Felix and Gretchen are here. We're having a traditional Mexican Christmas Eve feast, and it sure is good."

"I was afraid you'd be alone. I'm glad you're with friends."

"Me too."

"I have some good news, I think. I mentioned your case to a man at work a few weeks ago and he contacted a friend who's supposed to be influential in the Mexican government. Do you remember talking to anyone like that recently?"

"Just a strange man who came to my room."

"What do you mean?"

"I think I know who you're talking about."

"He says there's no question you'll be released. In fact, he guarantees he can get you out. What do you think?"

"You know how many times I've been told that someone can get me out. I'm still here. We can't put our faith in anyone, but ourselves."

"I agree, but I still try for miracles. Nothing has changed with the plan. Bill is still coming."

"Good."

"We're getting together tomorrow to work out the details and responsibilities."

"I feel good about everything. Whose coming with Billy?"

"Paul. He volunteered."

"Perfect."

Of all my friends on the list, I'd known Paul the longest. He was outgoing and friendly, honest and loyal; all the qualities you'd expect to find in a boy scout. The truth is, Paul was still a boy at heart. He played the flute, performed skits for kids, and brought joy into their lives. Prejudice was an unknown. God, goodness and the brotherhood of man were his guiding lights. He came from a French Catholic background and had studied to be a priest. He left the seminary for reasons he never wanted to talk about. Now, no less spiritual and lovingly called "the Bishop," he was into acting—happy, on track, and seriously involved with a lady. Why jeopardize all that on a risky adventure to rescue me when he could lose his freedom or his life? I didn't know the answer, but it felt great to have him in my corner.

The wheels of my chair seemed to float across the tiles as I made my way back to rejoin Gretchen and Felix. Everything was finally falling in place. This time we couldn't fail. On the way back to my room, I passed the guard slumped in his chair with his thermos of *ponche* on the floor. I could take off right now and no one would stop me. Except for the nurse on duty at the front desk, the corridor was deathly still. Gretchen and Felix would be told about the plan. I didn't want them to be seen around me and at risk after I was gone.

# 14

## *Escape*

It was late afternoon on December 30. I figured Paul and Bill had arrived and should be heading to their hotel from the airport. Felix had stopped by for the last time. I decided to write a welcome note outlining the details of my plan. I titled it after the book I had read in *Correcionales*.

PAPILLON BROS

Welcome to Mazatlân and the beginning of a great adventure. I'm sending my right-hand man, Felix, to give you torpedoes a rundown of the details. He will take you on a test run to make sure you know the safest route from here to the main highway. After that, it's a straight ride to Guadalajara.

Most important is getting out of the hospital. Best time would be after the guard change at eight pm. No one will be bringing any more food to the room, and as far as he knows, I'm sleeping. I've arranged that he be called to the front of the hospital for a few moments. I will quickly slip out in the wheelchair, close my door, and meet one of you in the courtyard. No alarm should go out until the next day. He doesn't even look into my room at night. Plan B is the same except it must be between 1 pm-3 pm when everything is super quiet. I need to know for certain so I can make sure the guard leaves. Contact me and let's confirm.

Please look as straight as everyone else here so they can't describe you easily. Let's have a full tank of gas, only. The driver can get tanked later. Keep your heads and hang onto your hats. Be ready for the ride of your lives.

Hasta mañana,

Sly Crow

Felix leaned over my shoulder. "Sly Crow?" he asked, puzzled.

I smiled. "Guess who's flying the coop."

Felix grinned.

I folded the note and handed it over. "Take this to the Papagayo Motel and give it to my cousin. If he's not there, wait for him. He and Paul may be at the car rental."

"OK." said Felix.

"Bill will probably be the inside man. He knows the hospital. They'll probably want you to show them the car routes right away. I don't know who'll be driving so make sure they both have it down."

"The best and fastest way south from here.?"

"Right. The less time we spend in this town the better."

Felix nodded. "I'll let you know how it goes."

I took his arm. "No. I don't want you coming back here."

"Why not?"

"They already know about you and me. If you're seen they might think you're in on this. Then I'd have to come back and break you out. Next time I see you, I'll be a free man. Stay far away from here and from me. Get yourself an alibi for tomorrow. Go back to Tabasco if you have to."

"But how will I know if . . ."

"I'll let you know. I'll be in touch."

"And if you need me?"

"We'll work it out on our own. You've done enough. We can't be seen together anymore. I've told Gretchen and Estela the same thing."

Felix looked away for a moment, not knowing what to say. Then he walked toward me and clasped my hand with both of his.

"Ay, Roberto, my thoughts and prayers will be with you. *Buena suerte!*"

"*Gracias mano.* I'll need good luck and more."

Felix struggled to smile. "I'd better get this to the Papagayo," he said, holding up the paper.

The long drive from Mazatlán to Guadalajara was my next concern. Estela had made the trip south to Nayarit on Christmas Eve with the checkpoints closed. I received another report, quite unexpectedly several days later when a small party of missionaries visited the hospital. They had just arrived from Guadalajara by bus. "I understand the ride takes a full day with all of the stops," I commented, discreetly as possible.

"It was enjoyable this time," a spokesman offered. "For once we came straight through. No roadblocks. Not one."

The all-important question had been answered. But would there be no roadblocks on New Year's Eve?

For Esperanza, the last day of the year began like many others. She carried in sheets and pillow cases and asked if I wanted my hair washed. She brought in hot water and soap and sponged off my body, massaged shampoo into my scalp. She brought my toothbrush, toothpaste and a small bowl. I brushed my teeth.

"OK, Roberto," she said, as she rolled my wheelchair near the bed. "Time for you to exercise."

This was the time I made my morning rounds of the hospital, happily greeting nurses and patients. Another wheelchair stroller named Paco often joined me and we soon became friends. His feet had been smashed by a passing train and he wasn't sure if he would ever walk again. Today we were upbeat and gave high fives as our wheelchairs passed from opposite directions. I continued to the very rear of the hospital, then reversed direction and rolled past the rear door. I had known for some time that this would be my escape route.

I was admiring the flowers and soaking up the Mexican sun in the patio when Esperanza stopped to tell me I had received a phone call. The party wouldn't give his name and refused to wait while she tracked me down. A minute later I was at the front desk dialing the Papagayo Motel and listening to a busy signal. Esperanza returned with more news. Mother Superior was waiting in my room for her lesson.

The Reverend Mother had just started her practice sentences when we heard a faint knock on the door. In stepped a familiar face with shaggy hair and a beard. My mouth dropped. I wasn't expecting to see Bill this early—and looking so grubby.

"I'm sorry," I said to the Mother. "This is my cousin Bill from California."

"Oh," the woman nodded gently. "I did not know you were having guests."

"Neither did I," I answered. My expression was far from joyous.

The Reverend Mother gathered her belongings and stood. "You will want to visit. I will return when you are not busy."

Bill held the door open. "Glad to have met you, Mother. I've heard a lot about you."

She looked at Bill strangely. But as she walked away, she was smiling.

"What's the matter with her?" Bill asked.

"She doesn't understand English very well," I answered. "Shut the door."

I sat up straight. "What the hell are you doing here. I told you not to come without calling first."

"We tried to call but ..."

"Why didn't you hold on—or call back? You know I can't go far in this place. Or did you think I was hang-gliding?"

"Hey, cool it. You're starting to act like the Bishop."

"All I've been thinking about are past screw-ups. Then you walk in."

"What's that supposed to mean?"

"It means everybody around here knows you from the last time. And why didn't you get rid of that beard?"

"Impossible. I couldn't because there wasn't any hot water this morning. I'm standing naked in a cold shower and I send the Bishop to the manager to get some hot water going. He returns with three Mexicans and ends up buying a blanket from them."

"What?"

"Forget it! Never send a Frenchman to explain something to a Mexican. It's been that kind of day, and I don't need you raising your voice at me."

"Look Cousin," my voice toning down, "all we need is for somebody to get suspicious. Did the guard spot you?"

"He was out by the front door having a smoke. And so what if he did? He's never seen me before."

"You're lucky, if he saw you now he wouldn't forget you."

Bill reached into his pocket and pulled out a small card. "Here," he said, handing it to me, "Maybe this'll help."

I looked at the color picture on the front. It showed Jesus standing with his arms outstretched, staring at me. "What's this for?" I asked.

"The Bishop's dropping them all over town. He figures if we keep our thoughts and energy pure and positive, this whole scene will come together for us."

"Jesus Christ!"

"Exactly."

"I hope he brought a stack of them."

"Well, it's like I told him. We might as well cover all the bets."

"That's for sure." I smiled. "But what's wrong? Why did you come?"

"When we got your note yesterday, Paul and I cracked up. I mean, it was really absurd. At such and such a time this had to happen, then the guard had to be distracted or it wouldn't work, then someone had to wheel you out, and the car had to arrive between this and that. There are only two of us, man. Not ten."

I sighed. "Billy... good vibes and positive thinking are great, but we can't afford to make a mistake that could have been prevented. My plan was to put the odds in our favor as much as possible."

"You got us so uptight, we thought... this is total insanity. So we agreed to try to forget it for a while and get drunk at the whorehouse. Trouble is, we couldn't really forget why we're here — or that the guns we see have real bullets in them. Paul couldn't even get a hard on."

"Good... He's going to need all of his strength for today. Where's he now?"

"Down at the beach."

"The beach?"

"Meditating. He's got this thing about St. Francis—a prayer that helps him."

I took a deep breath and closed my eyes. "What are you trying to tell me?"

"It's not off," Bill answered. "But we've got to move it up. And the sooner the better."

"God, everything is pointing to Plan B."

"Is that the one Felix told us about? Between one and three when the hospital's almost empty."

"Right, Cousin. We're going to need luck, prayers and any other help we can get because I have no idea when they'll discover me missing. One thing going for us is that it's New Year's Eve and even if they find me gone, everybody may be out celebrating."

"Let's do it. We'll go bananas if we have to wait until tonight."

"O.K. It's like playing a hunch, but everything is pointing toward a matinee. How does one-thirty sound?"

Bill checked his watch. "That gives me less than two hours to pick up Paul, pack our gear and get back."

"Maybe Paul should come in for me. Nobody's ever seen him before."

"He wouldn't know where to find you. He doesn't even know this place."

"Then I'll meet you in the patio—not here. If I'm not there, sit and wait. And try not to look anxious."

"In the patio at one-thirty sharp," Bill recited. "Be there or be square."

"We clasped hands as our eyes met. "This is it," I whispered as I felt the energy between us.

Time to put the last details of misdirection in place. Felix had brought me a road map of Mexico which I'd hidden in my nightstand drawer. I unfolded it quickly and laid it flat on the bed. Then, with a red marker, I drew lines heading north, circling certain cities along the route. Just before leaving, I'd place it in the trash can beside the bed. It was an old trick, but one that might work to buy us some time. Anything to try and throw the Federales off the track.

I was busily refolding the map when my door suddenly swung open. I turned in panic to find Gretchen staring at me.

"I know what you told me," she said, closing the door, "but I wanted you to have this." She offered a large bag of fresh fruit. "You'll want something to eat along the way."

I started to blow up, but laughed instead.

"What's so funny?" Gretchen asked.

"First Bill, now you. I suppose Felix will show up too."

"I'll only stay a minute."

"Everything's changed," I said. "Tonight's off."

"It's off?" she asked, shocked.

"We're leaving this afternoon. Bill and Paul don't want to wait—the pressure's getting to them."

"What about the guard?"

"What about him?"

Gretchen frowned. "He's sitting right outside."

"I figured he might be."

"I can get him away for you. He's been flirting with me for a couple of days. I'll get him to the front for a minute and you can get out of here."

"It's too early now, but if you can come back just before 1:30 and get him out for just a minute, I'll be gone before he gets back."

"That'll be fun. He likes me. I'll bring the flask and have an early New Year's toast out front with him."

"You're an angel, Gretchen. I'll never forget. See you back in the states with Cosey. Stay away from this place and lay low."

"Don't worry. I know nothing."

"Let Cosey and the guys know I won't forget them. I'll do everything I can to help when I'm free." One last hug and she was gone.

I had made a mental checklist of things to do. The map was ready, now the phone call. I wheeled to the front desk and placed a call to a hotel in Culiacán, which was north of Mazatlán. The map and the phone call would fit together like pieces in a puzzle. Could there be any doubt that I had headed northward in my escape? As I wheeled into my room and closed the door behind me, I noticed the guard sitting alertly on a chair facing my room.

Lunchtime was ending. Many patients took a siesta afterwards. Only two nurses would remain on duty; the others, along with the nuns, ate lunch in a room near the chapel behind the hospital. The guard on duty usually took a short break at this time. From my window, I often saw him outside the hospital entrance chatting with the neighborhood police or flirting with girls that walked by. Now with Gretchen coming, I had no doubt he would be outside at the right time.

When Esperanza arrived with my tray, I told her it wouldn't be necessary to bring food the rest of the day. "My cousin and some friends are coming shortly," I said. "They're stopping at a restaurant to pick up shrimp and chicken. We're all going to celebrate the new year together."

She looked at me oddly, but didn't argue. "Then you don't want to be disturbed?"

"That's right," I said. "In fact, I'll be keeping the door closed for our little celebration."

"I understand," she said, picking up the tray to leave.

Before she could reach the door, I stopped her. "Just a minute." I opened the nightstand drawer and pulled out a small box tied with ribbon. "I want you to have this."

Esperanza hesitated. "What is it for?"

"For being a friend and for taking such good care of me."

"But that's my job."

"I'd like to give you this present to remind you of my friendship when I'm gone." I started to set the box on the tray, but thought better of it. I placed it in the pocket of her uniform.

"Thank you for everything."

After she left, I began to get my things together. I made sure the misleading map was strategically located in the trash. Not too obvious, but easy enough to find. I picked up the book I had received from my grandmother for Christmas. The title bothered me, and I wondered if it was a sign: "You Can't Go Home Again" by Thomas Wolfe. I decided to take the book home with me. I placed the tourist visa with the name of Robert Martin, inside its pages. The visa, originally intended for the stretcher escape, had twenty days left before expiration. I placed a small box of my grandmother's fudge between my legs on the wheelchair. I left everything else so the room would look normal, still full of my belongings. Anyone looking in would think I was on one of my wheelchair strolls.

I was ready. I peeked out the window for the third time and felt the rush of adrenalin as I saw my uniformed guard near the entrance talking with another man. Gretchen was approaching them with smile on her face and a flask in her hand. It was time to make my move.

Bill was sitting on a bench with an older woman and two young children. He looked as nervous as I felt.

"Is everything ready?" I asked.

"Any time."

"Did you see the guard?"

"He walked outside as I was coming in." Bill smiled.

"You go first. Wait for me in the corridor. I'll follow casually."

"OK, I'll make sure the Bishop's where he's supposed to be."

Bill turned and walked down the hall. As he disappeared through the doorway, I began the longest ride of my life.

Suddenly a figure in blue popped out of the doorway. At that moment it felt like the floor had dropped out from under me. If it was the guard, I was done for. But it was a girl carrying an empty trash container back to the kitchen. She took no special notice of me as I rolled past her toward the second door.

Taking no chances, I wheeled five feet past the doorway to the hall's end, turned around and faced the long hallway I had just wheeled down. It was empty. Hallelujah! I cheered inside as Bill pulled me into the corridor.

"Paul was at the wrong door. I'm glad I checked," Bill said.

"So am I."

The wheelchair wouldn't fit through the outer door and Paul jumped out of the car and ran over to help.

"Close that door behind us," I told Bill. I didn't want to be seen by someone walking down the hall.

Paul greeted me with tough voice and curled upper lip from his latest stage play.

"Hello, sweetheart," he growled. "Remember that shirt of yours I loved so much? Well, I want it. I wouldn't want anyone to think I was doing this for nothin."

"Sure, it's yours. But who in the hell are you, anyway?"

"I've been Humphrey Bogart on stage for the last two months."

"Do you have a getaway car?"

"You better believe it."

"Then let's get out of here." I stood on one leg and placed an arm around each of their shoulders.

Bill and Paul held my cast-clad leg up and practically carried me in the air, setting me down gently in the rear of an open-doored red station wagon. I scooted back into the car as they returned for the wheelchair and accessories.

They were too late for the accessories. A youngster no older than twelve tossed my pillow and blanket into the wagon. He smiled, winked at me, and ran off.

"What's going on?" Bill asked. "Did you run an ad in the paper?"

"I've never seen him before in my life."

We looked at each other and shrugged.

I glanced across the street and saw a group of construction workers looking at us and our bright red station wagon. I began to wish that we had another car parked nearby to switch to for our long drive. This one stuck out like a fire engine.

The folded-up wheelchair landed beside me. I grabbed the blanket and covered both the chair and myself.

Paul jumped behind the wheel. Bill climbed in next to him.

Out of the corner of my eye I saw Felix with the kid that had helped us with the pillow and blanket. Both were standing on a corner of the street. The kid was bouncing a ball and Felix was waving his hat above his head. Was he saying goodbye or was it a warning?

"There's the guard." Bill said. "Hope he's not heading this way."

The guard was just about to turn the corner when Ramoncita and Estela stepped in front of him. Estela was smiling and talking to him while the little girl was pulling out a *buñuelo*.

"Are they covering for us?

"Beats the shit out of me," Paul answered! He jammed the key in the ignition and turned it. The motor roared.

"Looks like everybody I told to stay away did just the opposite… Incredible!

"Lie down, cover up with the blanket!" Bill said.

Paul stomped his foot on the accelerator. I heard the tires spin and grab the surface of the roadway. I raised my head to the window. We were moving, passing the staring faces of the construction workers that lined our route.

"*Adiós.*" I called out. They didn't hear me. It didn't matter. We were on our way!

# 15

## The Long Road

The red station wagon inched through the holiday traffic that choked the streets of Mazatlán. It was a glorious day under a cloudless sky, much like that afternoon nearly six months earlier when I arrived in the city with hopes and dreams for the future, a free soul. Now I was a fugitive, huddled under a blanket, afraid to be seen.

Even in mid-winter, the tropical sun was a potent force. It beat upon the roof of the car creating a sauna effect inside. The blanket added to the discomfort. We had been stuck in traffic for almost ten minutes. The hospital was still only blocks' away. Other than that, I was not really sure where we were. Apparently, neither were Paul and Bill. They bickered in the front seat over the turning point Felix had shown them. Paul swore it was at each corner we neared; Bill insisted we weren't even close.

As long as we kept moving, I felt fairly safe. But the snail-like pace was unnerving. I wanted to sit up, change positions, check surroundings. More than anything, I wanted to toss aside the suffocating blanket and dig into the suitcase for clothes that would transform my identity from runaway-hospital patient to tourist first-class.

Moving from the wheelchair to the wagon—and the maneuvering to get in back the car—had taken its toll. My leg throbbed. My shoulders ached. Muscles long asleep had been awakened too quickly. My mind remained sharp though, and Paul tested it right away.

"OK, Brother! I've got a question for you. If the alarm goes off, what's their first move?"

I had given the question a lot of thought, and I answered quickly,

"If any of the roadblocks are open, they'll be looking for us there. If they fall for my map trick, they'll began by looking north. We're heading south and I know the small towns in our direction with checkpoints. They probably won't be open today, but we can't be sure. Once we're across the Sinaloa state line, the odds are really in our favor."

Bill asked, "How long will it take us to get out of Sinaloa?"

"If Paul can drive as fast as my heart's pounding, about three hours."

Without warning, Paul turned sharply to the left. I lifted my head to find us heading toward oncoming traffic. We were on a one-way street, moving in the wrong direction. Bill and I hollered simultaneously—to the accompaniment of honking horns.

Paul quickly turned the steering wheel and the car spun around. I caught the wheelchair just as it slid against my hip.

"You've been screwing up since the plane landed," Bill said angrily.

"I found the highway, didn't I?" Paul countered. "We're just on the wrong side, that's all."

Bill sat straight in his seat, staring ahead. "Shit, you couldn't do a better job of getting picked up if you tried."

"Lay off," Paul said.

"All we need is for some cop to flag us down."

Paul silently finished the U-turn. Once again, we headed south—this time with the traffic flow.

"Very nice," Bill said, sarcastically.

"Hey, who's the flake who told the people at the airport rental we were taking the wagon to Guadalajara?"

"What?" I asked.

"I'll never get over that one," Paul said.

"Well, at least I didn't trip," Bill interrupted, "and fall down in the middle of the airport customs sending two ten-gallon gas cans down the aisle like bowling balls."

They went on and on. I didn't really hear what they were saying. I was thinking back to what seemed like ages ago, when all three of us were bachelors living on the beach—dreaming and raising hell. Bill and Paul were always bickering. It was their form of entertainment, playing one-upmanship. Their humor is unequaled, especially Bill's. They love each other. We love each other. Suddenly I felt good. But not for long. I startled myself and choked on the thought. Mother Superior. What if she comes back to my room? Damn!

Paul spoke, "Well, it's like I started to say before I was interrupted by a one-way street—I think you should listen to this and not worry about anything—we've got the "God-father" on our side. I'm crazy, I know, but listen—this really happened. I'm back there, idling, waiting for you two, nervous as hell. I reach for a cigarette and I find one Jesus card left… so I took it out and placed it on the dashboard, facing up. Next time I look up, the whole windshield has become a complete mirror reflection of Jesus. I felt covered, protected. You know what I mean?"

I listened to what he was saying and was feeling his excitement and confidence. I pulled some clothes from the suitcase. The road was narrowing, and the traffic was thinning.

Paul continued, "The more I stared at this reflection, the more I smiled. But in an instant, it changed from a mirror with Jesus to transparent glass, and I was looking directly into a little boy's eyes. He was standing at the corner bouncing a ball and looking right at me. He smiled, winked and turned to look along the hospital wall like he was watching for the guard. He could be an angel for all I know. One thing I'm . . ."

Bill interrupted, and his startled voice sent shivers up my neck. "The movie isn't over yet, Brother!"

I struggled to raise myself to see what was going on when Paul slammed on the brakes, throwing me violently forward with the chair flying on top of me. We were no longer moving. "Hey, what's going on?" I hollered.

"Shut up and pray," Paul hollered back.

"What the hell is . . ."

"Get down-flat," Bill said. "Under the blanket." There was panic in his voice.

I ignored him and turned toward the front. Through the glass I could see a long line of motionless vehicles surrounded by what looked like a small army of soldiers—carrying M-16 rifles.

"Dammit, get down!" Paul barked. "Hurry!"

I slumped to the back of the wagon, my mind in chaos. The alarm couldn't have gone out this fast, I told myself. We were barely out of the center of Mazatlán.

The wheel chair was a dead giveaway. I pulled it close to me and spread out the blanket. Now it was covered. So was I. All I could hear was labored breathing, my own, and that coming from the front seat. Then came random, isolated sounds. Approaching footsteps, slow and deliberate, moved across the gritty surface of the roadway. Somewhere, far away, I heard a motor. It grew progressively louder until it rumbled by. Then it disappeared and another took its place.

"I think we're OK," Bill said. "They're starting to let the trucks through."

"Where are the soldiers?" I wondered.

"Up the way," Paul answered. "Standing around—not doing anything."

The temptation to look was smothering me. "What's happening?" I asked. "What's . . ."

"Quiet," Paul said. "Don't move."

I lay hidden from view, listening to the huge trucks roll by. Then it was our turn and slowly we began to pull out.

"¡*Apúrate!*" a voice from outside ordered. "¡*Apúrate!*" Hurry up!

Paul stepped on the accelerator. Soon we were racing down a long stretch of highway, leaving slower vehicles in our wake. Looking back, I could see the trouble. A giant "semi-trailer" was on its side, blocking half the highway. The soldiers were directing traffic, first letting northbound travelers pass in the open lane, then southbound. So many soldiers. They had to have come from nearby. The logical assumption was that they'd been pulled from a checkpoint or the military camp.

The car rental agency had provided Bill and Paul with road maps of our route. I marked the areas of potential danger and drew a circle around the towns of Villa Union, Rosario and Esquinapa. Then there was the border, the Sinaloa-Nayarit state line.

Five miles out from Villa Union I spotted a police car on our tail. I had seen it earlier, but couldn't identify the markings until it had moved closer. I ducked under the blanket and yelled to the front seat. Paul watched it in the rear-view mirror.

"He'll get us for speeding," Bill said uneasily. "We're going too fast."

"Then why's he gaining on us?" Paul asked.

I could picture being cut off then held at gunpoint. "Where is he? What's he doing?" I wanted to know.

"Shut up and pray," Paul said with his stock answer.

We had an unofficial escort for three miles. Then Paul informed me the car was slowing, losing ground, and finally turned onto a dirt road. I threw the blanket aside and let out a warhoop. We had more to cheer about at Villa Union on seeing the shuttered checkpoint.

"One down, ten to go," Bill said with a touch of sarcasm in his voice.

"What's the next fear?" Paul asked.

I looked at my map. "Rosario," I said flatly.

The countryside had changed dramatically since leaving Mazatlán. We were fast approaching the sprawling Sierra Madres and the panorama sparked thoughts of the grizzly Bogart classic. The Bishop sat stone-faced at the wheel, his foot pinning the pedal to the floor. The speedometer indicated 160 kilometers—about 100 miles an hour.

We ascended into the foothills without noticeable loss of speed, despite the serpentine road. By the time we neared the crest, however, we were barely moving in low gear. A truck, struggling to make the climb, was in our way. Unable to pass, we were forced to hover in the cloud of smoke that poured from its exhaust.

At last, we were on the downgrade and the road ahead was straight and clear. Here was our chance to move out. Paul turned the wheel and stepped on the gas. Suddenly, as we were next to the truck, we heard a screech. The driver had slammed on the brakes and his massive vehicle was swerving uncontrollably from side to side. At that instant we saw a cow in our path, momentarily standing in a confused state then bounding for the soft shoulder and safety. Paul hit the brakes as it ran in front of us. We heard a light "thunk" as its tail struck the front fender and we swerved off the road, bumping and skidding over rocks and loose gravel. Paul had his hands full trying to maneuver the wagon. Bill was hanging on for dear life, and I had more than I could handle in the back. The wheelchair went flying along with the suitcases and the blanket-covered mound behind me. Surprisingly, we made it back on the main road again, speeding toward Rosario. I tossed back the covering to find two gas drums taped tightly together. They had filled them up driving in from the airport. It was our emergency fuel supply, over thirty dollars-worth of gasoline.

The approach to Rosario was marked by road signs indicating the number of kilometers to the town. We watched the figure dwindle. There was nothing to do but stare ahead and hope we wouldn't see a group of soldiers with M-16s waiting to greet us. We let out a cheer as we quickly passed the town without a reception committee.

Esquinapa was our next hurdle. It had been over two hours since the breakout. Every passing minute meant the odds were increasing that someone would discover my disappearance. One telephone call and the state police might be on the alert.

There was no roadblock in Esquinapa either.

"We're going to make it," Bill yelled. "We're really going to make it!"

No one contradicted him, but I wouldn't let out my first big sigh of relief until we left Sinaloa. Paul looked at his watch as we approached the Sinaloa-Nayarit state line. We were right on schedule and making great time. I had thought I was being optimistic when I told him we could make Nayarit in three hours. We crossed the state line without incident and as we cheered, I realized our main obstacle was behind us.

The climate and terrain of Nayarit was semi-tropical. Lush green foliage and flowering trees greeted us as we approached Tepic, the capital. There we would stop for gas and switch drivers. We checked the road signs. There were two main roads coming up, leading in different directions. We had to be careful not to head towards Puerto Vallarta, rather than Guadalajara.

We pulled into a large gas station for our well-earned pit stop. The number of gas pumps and large spaces between them indicated this was a major truck stop. On the right was a gift shop manned by a little boy who approached as Bill and Paul got out to stretch their legs.

We had planned to stop in Tepic just long enough for Bill and Paul to trade places. The young entrepreneur had other ideas. He ran to us carrying a huge bamboo cage in his arms. A tropical bird sat placidly inside, its colorful streaming feathers spread in a magnificent display.

"You want?" the youngster asked in Spanish. "You buy?"

Bill squatted to take a closer look: "How much?" he asked.

"Cow shit," Paul blurted.

Bill gave him an ugly look.

"Cow shit," Paul said again. "It's all over the fender. That poor cow really dropped a load on us back there. Can't say I blame her."

Bill took a look. "You scared the shit out of her."

"*Vámonos*," I hollered from my bed inside the car. "Let's go!"

Bill was tapping on the side of the cage, trying to trigger a reaction from the bird. Paul joined him.

"You want?" the young Mexican asked again.

Jeez! I mumbled in disgust. Now they'll probably want to hear it say something.

"Does it talk?" Bill asked the boy.

"Forget the damn bird," I shouted.

Bill glared at me. "Give us a minute to unwind, for God's sake!"

"You can unwind when we get home," I shot back. "This isn't a sightseeing tour."

"Robert's right," Paul said. "We're wasting time. Let's get the gas."

A few minutes later Bill climbed in behind the wheel. Soon we were racing toward a sight so spectacular that all else paled by comparison. The sun was setting and the sky was fired with reds, pinks, and oranges; hot colors that stretched from the mountains to the ocean—an ever-changing palette that grew more breathtaking as the seconds passed.

"It's a sign," the Bishop said reverently. "The gods are with us."

Paul spoke with such conviction I expected to hear a chorus of angels. I didn't, of course. But I knew that Paul had arranged for thousands of worshipers to pray for us on this day.

The sky turned dark quickly. We sped along an unlit treacherous highway, over rolling hills covered with dense tropical vegetation. Occasionally, on the outskirts of a remote village, we spotted life in our headlights: a stray dog, a lone human balancing produce on a head-basket, an underfed burro.

By the time we left Nayarit and entered the State of Jalisco, we were nauseous from breathing gas fumes. The drums at my elbow were far from airtight. We had opened all the windows in the wagon and sat with throbbing heads and queasy stomachs, chilled to the bone.

The gauge on the dashboard indicated plenty of fuel remained, more than enough to get us to our destination. Knowing that, we were ready to toss the leaky drums overboard. But they were probably worth decent money for a poor family in Mexico.

"Why don't we just drop them off on somebody's porch?" Bill said humorously.

Paul's face lit up. "Great idea, Bill."

Bill spotted a distant light and pulled off the side of the highway. I started to tell him to keep driving, but hesitated when I saw those two bright faces. I had to smile to myself as I watched them tiptoe to a small farm-house carrying the gas cans, and run back to the car laughing like little kids.

Magdalena was the only checkpoint after Sinaloa that worried me. It was the largest and most thorough checkpoint between Mazatlán and Guadalajara. It was also the most permanent; it rarely closed. But this was New Year's Eve. I hoped that if it was open, no one had received word of my escape. After all, I was not on the most wanted list and nobody expected me to head south. We cruised through Magdalena an hour before midnight, heady with a sense of victory. The only reception we got were the whoops and smiles of revelers.

We had hoped to slip into Guadalajara unnoticed in the boisterous carnival atmosphere. My mother had made advance reservations at the Hotel Genoa. We were to remain at the hotel until we headed for our flight the next morning. But the maps we had were useless; not one listed the address where the hotel was located. Even if they had, there were no street signs anywhere. Lost from the start, Bill drove around in circles through the crowded downtown area until we had no choice but to ask a group of pedestrians for directions.

Minutes later, on the main boulevard, Bill failed to see the small white flag protruding from an open manhole. The left front wheel plunged into a gaping hole, throwing us forward and stopping traffic. Fortunately, we had enough momentum to bounce out of the opening. But now we attracted the unwanted attention we had hoped to avoid.

Pedestrians and drivers stared at us. The wheel was damaged so severely it was difficult to drive in a straight line. The sleek station wagon was now covered with dust and dung. Worse, it bucked, chugged, and twisted as it crept along the downtown thoroughfare barely under Bill's control. It was all he could do to hang on to the throbbing steering wheel.

We had gone barely two blocks when the car stalled. "I've had it!" Bill announced bluntly. He had been driving for hours.

We were in the right lane and the traffic stopped behind us, horns blaring while waiting to move into the next lane. Paul didn't waste any time switching places with Bill, but as he opened the door to the driver's side, a woman and young girl approached him. The short, brown skinned woman, wrapped in a serape extended her hand out while the little girl held up some trinkets. Paul chose one and put some pesos in the woman's hand.

"Gracias, señor," she said, as their faces lit up in smiles.

He sat down in the driver's seat and reached back and handed me the trinket.

"Got to keep the good energy flowing."

I opened my hand and was staring at a pendant with the image of La Virgen de Guadalupe. I immediately thought of Estela.

It was near midnight and Paul got us moving again, barely chugging along. The city was taking on a frenzied air. Men and women, boys and girls were dancing in the streets as groups of strolling mariachis played with passion. Firecrackers were exploding around us and sirens wailed. One of the screaming sirens belonged to a police car that carried a flashing signal on its roof. It was directly behind us.

My mouth went dry as Paul slowed to a stop. "Remember, we're just tourists," I said. "Play dumb." Then I covered my leg.

A man in black slowly stepped toward us.

"Smile," I said. "Look happy. It's New Year's Eve."

"Whoopee," Bill mumbled as he twirled his finger in the air.

The officer walked to the front of the car then back to Paul's window. He had an amused look on his face. "Trouble?" he asked.

"*Sí*," we each answered at split-second intervals.

"*Turistas?*"

"*Sí*," we answered again. We looked like goons bobbing our heads and smiling.

"Where from?" he asked.

No one wanted to answer.

"Where from?" he repeated.

My palms were wet. Finally, I said, "California."

The officer stepped again to the front of the car. It was the twisted wheel that had his attention.

"How did you damage the wheel?" he asked.

"A big hole in the road," I said quickly. "Outside town. We nearly turned over."

"You were fortunate," he said. "You should not be driving this damaged car. It is much too dangerous with so many people in the streets."

"We'll be careful," I said.

The officer smiled. "I could fine you but . . . well ... it is New Year's Eve."

I wrapped my fingers around a bill in case he changed his mind.

"We're looking for our hotel," Bill said. "The Genoa."

The officer checked the street. "Wait here," he said sharply. Then he was back in his car, pulling in front of us and motioning for us to follow.

We drove through the teeming streets of Guadalajara, behind the patrol car with red lights flashing past the Degollado Theater and the Government Palace, turning left one block and right another, until we spotted the marquee of the Hotel Genoa up ahead. "This is unreal," Paul said. "One minute we're running from them, the next they're helping us."

"If word gets out during the night, every cop in town will know where to find us." Bill said.

"Then why don't we wait til this guy leaves," Paul said, "then move to another place?"

"Relax, I don't think they'll be looking in Guadalajara. I called a hotel in Culiacan from the hospital and made a reservation. Anyway, between Jesus and the Virgin, I get the feeling were protected."

"There's something else," Bill said, his voice cracking.

Paul held up his hand. "Save it. We've got enough problems for now."

"It's the plane tickets and my visa," Bill said, rummaging around the front seat. "They're gone."

# 16

## *Happy New Year*

Suddenly the night sky was filled with diamonds of multicolored lights. Explosions rumbled and church bells chimed. It was midnight, the New Year, 1976. Our Bicentennial was just beginning.

"They didn't have to go to all that trouble for us," Paul said glowingly, "I wonder if the celebration comes with the room."

"Mom always finds the best deals," I laughed.

We had arrived at the Hotel Genoa with little fanfare. Our police escort pulled in, got out of his car, and walked to our window.

"*Feliz Año Nuevo,*" he said, wishing us Happy New Year with a smile.

"Happy New Year," the three of us answered in unison.

While Paul was checking in, Bill found the missing tickets and visas. "Don't tell Paul," he smiled and handed them to me.

Now safe in our room, we were enjoying the tacos and beer Paul and Bill had picked up at a small restaurant down the street.

"I wish we had more time to spend here under different circumstances," Bill said, gulping down some beer. "That mariachi music down the street was the best Mexican music I've heard. It came from the soul; it had *duende*. And those cobblestone streets. . . the sunset in Nayarit. Damn, I never knew this part of Mexico."

"Those are some of the things that always brought me back, cousin. Maybe it's Mexico's way of saying goodbye to us."

"Here's to Mexico," Paul lifted his beer, "Hello and Goodbye."

"Ole," Bill and I joined in.

"I'm going to shower down," Bill said, as he set down his empty bottle.

Paul began ransacking through the luggage as soon as Bill was out of the room.

"What in the world are you looking for?" I asked.

"Nothing. Nothing important," Paul said, as his forehead creased in disbelief. "Only the plane tickets your cousin misplaced."

"You mean these." I pulled them out of my pocket like magic.

"All right, you found them, or did you have them all the time?"

"No. I ..."

"Hey, listen," Paul interrupted. "Don't tell Bill. Let him sweat for a while. Where'd you find them?"

"Bill found them in the car while you were checking us in. He told me not to tell you."

"What? Why that dirty bastard. This is no time to play games."

"You were going to do the same thing."

"Well, shit! That's still no goddamn excuse." We both broke into laughter.

Paul shook his head and said, "I'm beat. I'm going to lay down until he gets out of the shower. It takes him forever. By the way, don't let on that I know about the tickets."

An hour passed before Bill was out of the shower. Paul had gone downstairs to get cigarettes.

"Where's Paul?" Bill asked.

"He went to get some cigarettes and take one more look for the tickets." We both smiled.

The door opened and Paul walked in. "Guess what I found?" Paul held the tickets in the air, "Viola! They were wedged between the seats. I guess they fell in when we hit a bump—or something."

Bill smirked at the indirect reference to the open manhole. He looked in my eyes. They were a dead giveaway. At that moment we all knew what the other knew and laughed in unison.

"I propose a toast," Paul said, quickly pulling out a steel flask from his bag. I've been saving this blessed drink for just such an occasion. Chartreuse, a liqueur made with 130 herbs by the Carthusian Monks. Still made by my family for the Christmas holidays." He filled our cups. "This is more than a drink, it's an experience."

"Here's to the morning —the final lap home."

"To home sweet home," I joined.

He was right, it was like nothing I had ever consumed before. Amazing.

Bill took a long swig. "Amen brothers. You know the Chinese have a saying . . .

When heaven is about to confer

A great office upon a man,

It first exercises his mind with suffering

and his sinews and bones with toil.

It exposes him to poverty

and confounds all his undertakings.

Then it is seen if he is ready."

We finished our Chartreuse and called it a night. We would try to get a few hours' sleep. There was an alarm clock in Bill's suitcase and I had requested a wake-up call, just in case. Neither were necessary.

I was awake long before sunrise. Too many things kept preying on my mind, much to be done before leaving for the airport. I wheeled into the bathroom. Along with a fresh change of clothes, Mom had packed a razor, scissors, a box containing black hair coloring solution, and an eye patch. I slipped the patch over my head then pulled it off. If anything, it would draw more attention to me. I snipped away at my mustache, getting as close to the skin as I could with the scissors. Then I lathered up my face and shaved clean.

The hair coloring instructions sounded easy enough. Just shampoo in, the flyer read. But there was no way I could get my head under a faucet and I certainly didn't have time to fool with lotions and toners or make a "skin patch" test. Anyway, what the hell, I thought. If they're waiting for an escapee in a wheelchair with a broken left leg, none of this junk is going to help. I decided to forget the hair dye and concentrate on looking neat and classy. I put on the top of my blue leisure suit and Bill helped slip the bottoms over my leg and cast.

We left for the airport at six thirty a.m., three hours before the plane was scheduled to take off. Traffic on the roads was nil, but we expected that. After all, it was New Year's Day. The locals had nothing to do but sleep off the excesses of the night before. There were no bowl games or New Years' day parade to get them stirring.

We still weren't out of the woods. The bright red station wagon came to mind and the fact they had given our final destination as Guadalajara at the rental kiosk. If someone reported the suspicious activity at the rear of the hospital and described the car, it might be easy to find out where the vehicle had come from. After all, I had never seen anything that remotely resembled our "fire engine" anywhere in my previous travels.

Paul parked the station wagon as far from the car rental as possible. From there we made our way to the terminal.

"What should we do about the wagon?" Bill asked. It was a question that was on all our minds.

"I'll take the keys back," Paul said.

"What would happen if we didn't," Bill asked.

"That might set off negative vibes," Paul said. "We've got to keep this trip on a positive level."

"They could get us for the damage," Bill said.

"We paid for the insurance, remember . . . I'll charge in at the last minute. In and out real fast, you know?"

The entrance to the terminal building was only a few feet away.

"This is almost as much fun as waiting for you outside the hospital yesterday," Paul said. "Have you noticed all the people who don't look like they're going anywhere? Plainclothes types, if you know what I mean."

I'd thought the same thing. "It's just your imagination," I said.

Paul held open the terminal door as Bill pushed me inside. A dozen or so people milled about, not counting the airline employees and the clean-up crew.

Bill checked his watch. "We've got nothing but time to kill."

"There must be someplace we can go where we won't be so obvious."

"I'm the problem," I said. "I'm the one they'll be looking for."

Without a word, Bill wandered off. A few minutes later he was hustling me into a dim recess beneath the staircase leading to the second floor.

"This looks safe," he said. "Wait here while we take care of the tickets and luggage."

No sooner had they gone than I began to doubt the wisdom of Bill's thinking. What would I say if anyone saw me? What was I doing under the stairs? Didn't I look more suspicious than ever? Perhaps if I were more visible, I wouldn't seem to be hiding. And I would feel less claustrophobic. I released the brakes and inched forward just as two uniformed men, security police carrying walkie-talkies, came into view. My heart began to pound furiously. When they passed without seeming to notice me, I let out a sigh of relief.

It was forty-five minutes before Bill and Paul returned. They had spent the extra time wandering, checking for suspicious looking characters. By now, everyone looked suspicious. Our minds were playing tricks. The boarding area was on the second floor and the building was without an elevator.

"We'll have to carry you up in the chair," Bill said, "a step at a time. There's no other way."

I wondered if the gods were really on our side. Lately, we couldn't make a move without being thrown in the spotlight.

It was nearly eight thirty when we reached the upper level. "They'll be letting us board soon," Paul said, catching his breath. "I'd better drop off the car keys."

"You're sure you want to do that?" Bill asked.

"I am," Paul nodded. "I won't be gone long."

He started to leave when I stopped him.

"Be careful! We don't know if an alarm went out. If they're looking for the car, they may try to stall you until the Feds arrive. Tell them you're staying at the Fiesta Americana hotel if they need a contact number and get outta there…fast."

"Fiesta Americana…got it!"

"And if we're still here when you come back, act like you don't know us."

Paul looked at me strangely.

"This is our last test," I said. "It's better if we split up—at least 'til we're on the plane."

"Are you sure?" Paul asked.

"If anything happens, you'll still be free. We may both need you."

"Oh . . . well," Paul sputtered. "I'll be ready if I'm needed."

Outside, on the runway, a Mexicana Airlines jet was taxiing into position near the boarding ramp. We watched and waited. And waited.

Bill and I had been joined by a fair-sized crowd of travelers and well-wishers at the observation window. Now a part of the group was breaking away to form a line at the embarking point.

"Here," Bill said, handing me an envelope, "you might need this."

I slipped the boarding pass in my pocket as a foreign voice from the P.A. system quieted the chattering crowd. The Mexicana Airlines flight for Los Angeles, it announced, was ready to board.

My heartbeat quickened. "Looks like this is it," I said apprehensively.

Bill gave the wheelchair a shove and we started toward the swelling line. "I don't see Paul," he said.

I didn't either—only a man in a blue uniform. He was looking directly at me, coming my way. Uh-oh.

He said simply, "Robert Marteen?"

The name didn't register. The man leaned close and smiled.

"Robert Marteen?" he asked again, this time in an almost subservient way.

A finger jabbed at my back. "This is Robert Martin," Bill said.

I looked at Bill blankly. His head was nodding.

"Oh, yes," I said, without conviction. "I'm Robert Martin." Then I noticed an airline insignia on the pocket of the man's jacket and relaxed.

"Follow me, please," he said in Spanish. "You'll be boarded first because of your condition." Bill pushed me past the line of waiting travelers toward the plane. Once inside we were met by a corps of attendants. I felt like visiting royalty.

Mom had purchased five seats for the flight, three for me alone so I could sit sideways with my leg extended. The airline attendants had everything waiting—arm rests removed, pillows arranged, blankets and magazines handy. All that remained was to lift me from the wheelchair to the waiting "throne" and tie me in. By the time the other passengers started to board I was comfortably settled. Across the aisle Bill sat alone, the seat to his right, still unoccupied.

"What time is it?" I asked.

"Nine-twenty," he answered.

The plane was twenty minutes late. I knew Federales were stationed at all major airports. I hoped they were getting a late start or had the day off. I was surely reported missing by now. I wished the plane would take off. But first, Paul? What happened to Paul? Where is he? I looked down the aisle again and this time I spotted him. If I hadn't known better, I'd have thought he'd just left a sauna. He was sweating profusely and looked tense. When he reached us, he relaxed and let a breath of air out.

"Oh, man, I am so high," he said reaching his seat.

"What happened?"

"The woman in front at the rental office told me to wait. She said the manager needed to speak with me. She looked nervous. Something didn't feel right. I told her the manager could call me at the Fiesta Americana and got out fast… almost bumped into three men in the hallway heading to the rental office. One of them with a scar gave me a nasty look. I went out the front door and hopped in a taxi to the Fiesta Americana. Just as we got out of the airport, I told the driver I forgot my briefcase, and to take me back."

"Jesus, Paul. Sounds like Jefe and the boys. Good thing they've never seen you. Those prayers must be working," I told him.

As long as we were in Mexico, or over it, there was danger. The *Federales* could force the plane to land, if they discovered I was on board before we reached the border.

"Is everything all right, Mr. Martin?" one of the attendants stopped to ask.

"Fine," I answered. "How soon are we taking off?"

I heard the door slam shut. "Right away," was the answer.

We were moving, slowly pulling away from the terminal and heading for the runway. Now the engines roared. The plane shook and I felt myself being pressed against the seats. I looked out the window. We were airborne!

None of us said much over the next two hours, but we were all anxious to get out of Mexican airspace. When the pilot announced that we were entering the United States, we raised our glasses and let out a big "Happy New Year".

It was ten-forty a.m. when the plane landed at Los Angeles International Airport. We had yet to roll to a stop, but Bill and Paul were already standing.

A stewardess told them to be seated. "You need to wait until all the passengers have gone," she said.

Across the aisle, Bill and Paul exchanged frowns. I settled back uneasily as the plane began to empty. Then we were alone with one of the attendants. He had my wheelchair, pushing it into position close to me. We were led from the plane down a special ramp where two men were waiting. They identified themselves as customs officials. They singled Paul out for questioning.

"Are you with the man in the wheelchair?" one of them asked.

Paul stopped abruptly. It was easy to see what was flashing through his mind. Bill and I felt it too. We were hoping the Mexicans hadn't found out I was on the plane and alerted the US authorities. If this was our final moment of truth, Paul faced it openly and with great faith.

"Yes," he answered with conviction, "he's my best friend. He's had an accident and we're bringing him home to his parents."

"I understand," the man said. "Maybe we can cut a few corners for you. Follow us, please."

Paul turned and winked. Bill and I breathed easier.

In a small room adjacent to the baggage claims area the customs men checked Bill's and Paul's identification. Then it was my turn. All I had was my phony birth certificate. I had memorized the birth date, place of birth and mother's maiden name. I was concentrating so hard on remembering these details that I inadvertently said Robert Miller, when he asked me my name.

"Robert who?" the customs man asked.

"Robert Martin," I said confidently, hoping he'd think he heard me wrong the first time.

"OK, go out that door," the official said, pointing the way, "and pick up your baggage."

Passengers were waiting in line to have their luggage inspected.

"I'll take care of the bags," Paul offered. "Go ahead and get Robert out of here."

Bill didn't have to be told twice. We cruised through the inspection area and out the door as fast as Bill could push me. Nobody stopped us.

Immediately outside I saw a familiar face—laughing, crying.

"Robby."

"Mom."

She hugged me tightly. "I knew you'd make it. I knew it!"

The nightmare was over. I was home… Our smiles outshone the sun!

# Epilogue

My story ends with a touch of irony.

Months after the escape on New Year's Day, I learned that my "*absuelto*" (not guilty papers) had been delivered to the prison on December 27. For some reason, perhaps because of the holidays, they were never forwarded to the hospital. My release day had been set for January 6th. I never found out who was responsible for this, but I had my suspicions.

I could not forget my friends who remained in prison and I wanted to do everything possible to help them. I was in a position to make their situation known all over America through the publicity of my escape in a wheelchair. I was immediately approached by many news entities in the US and consented to a number of interviews to make public the plight of my fellow Americans remaining in Mexican jails. Fearing my possible extradition back to Mexico, we set up escape routes from each interview. Hotels were booked under my mother's name and I moved frequently. Too expensive. Soon she found an apartment close to home, where I could recuperate and my leg would heal.

I want to acknowledge the courageous acts by the mothers of prisoners in Mexican jails that formed a group 1732 Inc to fight for their children and work with our government to help pass the Prisoner Exchange Treaty. They arranged many interviews for me with newspapers, magazines, and television. For almost a year Paul worked actively with this group. Taking their name from a law that grants the President authority to act in behalf of U.S. citizens in foreign countries, families banded together on behalf of their children to pressure the government to ensure fair treatment for Americans held as prisoners in Mexico.

It was through 1732, Inc. that I was invited to testify before the Senate Judiciary Committee in July, 1977.

I told part of my story there.

A few months later the United States and Mexico signed a Prisoner Exchange Treaty and some American prisoners chose to come home.

Paul give me a framed copy of the prayer he read on the beach in Mazatlán prior to the escape. The Bishop is no longer with us, but his favorite prayer is always close to me.

### PRAYER OF ST FRANCIS

Lord make me an instrument of your peace
Where there is hatred, let me sow love
Where there is injury, pardon
Where there is doubt, faith
Where there is despair, joy
Where there is darkness, light
Where there is sadness, joy

O Divine Master, grant that I might not so much
seek to be consoled as to console
To be understood as to understand
To be loved as to love
For it is in giving that we receive
It is in pardoning that we are pardoned
And it is in dying that we are born to eternal life

# Appendix

Robert Miller appeared on Good Morning America, 60 Minutes, and was featured in People Magazine.

He was invited to testify before the Senate Sub-Committee considering the Prisoner Exchange Treaty between the United States and Mexico.

TESTIMONY BEFORE
U.S. SENATE JUDICIARY COMMITTEE,
JULY 14, 1977

STATEMENT OF ROBERT MILLER, MANHATTAN BEACH,
CALIFORNIA

Senator Joe Biden is asking the questions:

**Mr. Miller.** My name is Robert Miller. I represent myself as a former prisoner in Mexico.

In fact, I was in prison with Robert Quirk. You have heard statements from his parents already about the conditions and about what he went through. I can attest to the validity of their statements.

I had been in the Mazatlán prison for two weeks at the time of his arrival. He was in pretty bad shape physically and mentally. He is a young kid. He is a good kid.

**Senator Biden.** How old are you?

**Mr. Miller.** I am 32.

I do not want to repeat a lot of things that have already been mentioned about the prison. I have those in my statement.

I might talk about Hurricane Olivia which was mentioned where prisoners were buried alive. I was one of the prisoners buried alive. I was dug out by my fellow prisoners. I broke two bones and was taken to a hospital where I spent a week without any treatment whatsoever, until my mother arrived to put up some money and exert pressure for an operation.

I have been physically disabled for a year and a half. Finally, I am on my feet again and fortunately back home.

**Senator Biden.** How long have you been out of prison?

**Mr. Miller.** I escaped New Year's Eve of 1975. That was from the hospital.

**Senator Biden.** What had you been arrested for?

**Mr. Miller.** At the time I was apprehended I was not charged for a week. When they finally charged me, it was for the possession of one marijuana cigarette, which they expressed, according to my attorney, in milligrams of marijuana.

**Senator Biden.** How long were you sentenced?

**Mr. Miller.** I was not sentenced. I had been incarcerated for six months. I found out, only after escaping, that I had been found not guilty but that the papers had been taken to the prison four days before my escape instead of being delivered to the hospital where I was a patient. In fact, Robert Quirk was called down in my place before they found the mistake, that the papers were actually for my release.

At the time I escaped I figured I was facing a minimum penalty of five years and three months.

The doctor had told me that he was going to transfer me back to the prison although I was unable to walk or get around myself.

**Senator Biden.** Have you gone to trial?

**Mr. Miller.** No. The system is different in Mexico. I was taken to an office in to make statements before the judge's secretary. The judge reads your statement, looks at the write up from the Prosecutor and he makes a decision, hopefully within six months. You never actually see a court in Mexico.

**Senator Biden.** Please proceed.

**Mr. Miller.** I am one of the fortunate few to have returned to a country where human rights and due process of law are more than just words. The hundreds of suffering Americans still imprisoned in Mexican jails, living under the worst conditions imaginable, are desperately in need of the spark of hope that only their government can provide—the knowledge that their country still cares.

The story of my arrest is fairly typical. I was on my way to the highly respected Institute Allende to continue my studies when apprehended in Mazatlán for reasons I must guess at even now. My car was literally torn apart and I was searched and humiliated. My companion, a local resident, was released immediately. Nothing illegal was found in my possession or in the car, but I was subsequently beaten, tortured, and held incommunicado for seven days. I was not even allowed to make a phone call or contact the American Consulate.

When I was finally permitted to speak with a Mexican attorney, he informed me that I would be charged with possession of one marijuana cigarette unless he received $5,000 to pay off government officials.

Naturally, my mother wanted to do everything possible to obtain my release. To raise funds, she eventually had to mortgage her home. Shortly after receiving the money, the attorney took himself off the case.

I was told that a new drug law had recently been passed by the Mexican legislature with pressure from the United States. Under this law I was facing a minimum sentence of five years and three months. The law did not differentiate between marijuana or heroin, possession or trafficking.

I was first imprisoned in a military camp outside Mazatlán, then transferred to a sweat tank in the town's central jail. From there I was sent to the main prison, the notorious Cárcel Publico Municipal. Conditions were appalling. Everyone was sick with something—from minor discomforts such as diarrhea and scabies, to hepatitis, tuberculosis, and typhoid. Maintaining our health, mental and physical, was constantly on our minds. To survive, it had to be.

Everything costs money in a Mexican jail and most of the American prisoners relied on money from home in order to live. After our mail was withheld for weeks, we signed a petition delivered to the American Consulate and had our parents contact their congressmen to have it resumed. If you don't want to sleep among bodies and rats on the crowded cement of the prison yard, you can purchase a cot. But you must also buy a space to put the cot. If that space is protected from the heat and rain, it will cost more. The charge to buy a key to the toilet is $16 and it is $8 to make a collect telephone call. Food, of course, is a major expense. There are many others.

I mentioned that outside money is essential in order to live. For many, it is used to perpetuate a living death. Entering the main prison in Mazatlán, newcomers are met by a commission, its members being old-time, hardened prisoners. This select group makes the rules for day-to-day living and enforces them. The commission makes much of its money by introducing nervous, young Americans to hard drugs. Extortion is another one of their techniques. Heroin, they tell us, will calm the nerves and make time less painful.

For those who do not have ready cash, credit is available. When checks and money grams arrive from home, they are often confiscated to pay for past and future purchases. Drugs of various kinds are readily available. I know of one American who smoked marijuana for the first time inside a Mexican prison. And I saw some Americans, young people who were arrested for minor possession of marijuana, who were persuaded to use harder drugs for the first time and became heroin addicts.

It is not easy to be optimistic in a Mexican prison. Many Americans have simply given up hope after being taken for large sums of money by unscrupulous Mexican attorneys, being let down by their country's local representatives, and being subject to continual harassment and oftentimes barbaric tortures.

These Americans are far from home and loved ones and are a greatly outnumbered minority. Some are desperate enough to risk their lives in escape rather than be subjected to this inhumane treatment for over five years. I was that desperate.

I must emphasize that it is not only imprisoned American men and women who are experiencing this nightmare. The suffering extends across the border as well, to families of prisoners. They not only share the pain of their children, but are losing huge sums of money—money that they can ill afford to spend. These people need your help with this treaty almost as desperately as their sons and daughters.

Today there are over 600 Americans in Mexican jails and the number is increasing. The majority are not involved with major narcotic syndicates trafficking in hard drugs. When I was in prison there was not one American arrested for possession of heroin. Some of these so-called criminals are simply kids on vacation in Mexico who wind up becoming heroin addicts in Mexican jails. Valuable lives are being ruined. There can be no rehabilitation under these conditions.

Although the prisoner exchange treaty is a positive step in the right direction, we must look beyond it to the basis for the dramatic increase in arrests of American citizens in Mexico. When did we initiate this cooperative drug policy with Mexico that puts a bounty on Americans? How many times in peace time have there been over 600 Americans in a foreign prison? Are we really stopping the major drug traffickers, or are young amateurs being used as pawns in a political chess game?

If it is within the realm of human possibility, I urge you to bring these Americans home and give them the chance they need so desperately. I hope this treaty will be the first positive step in re-evaluating our drug policy with Mexico. We have a chance to show the world that we are not only concerned with human rights when it comes to other nations, but we are also deeply concerned with human rights of Americans in foreign countries.

**Senator Biden.** Thank you very much.

What additional steps would you suggest? You mentioned a first step. Do you have any suggestions for a second step and a third step?

**Mr. Miller.** I believe that the new Mexican drug law was put into effect through American pressure equating minor possession of marijuana with possession of quantities of heroin and harder drugs. I believe we can put pressure through our State Department and the President, probably not through the Congress itself, to communicate with Mexico on possibly a new law or retracting the old law that was passed through pressure of our administration. Possibly Congress through funds in the foreign aid program can have some power. I know that we give Mexico quite a number of dollars in foreign aid. Maybe this money is being used to train Mexican Federales and so on.

**Senator Biden.** Mr. Miller, what do you consider a minor possession of marijuana? Do you consider 30 kilos a minor possession of marijuana?

**Mr. Miller.** I believe in Mexico that yes, I would consider that a minor offense, the smugglers deal in much larger quantities. I would not consider it minor in the United States. Many of the Mexicans feel that a ton is the normal number.

**Senator Biden.** How about in terms of it being transported into the United States?

**Mr. Miller.** Actually being transported? In the act of transportation?

**Senator Biden.** Yes.

**Mr. Miller.** As I say, in Mexico again I think most Mexicans consider it minor. However, in the United States it probably would be considered major.

**Senator Biden.** Would you suggest that marijuana should not even be a consideration? You say comparing minor amounts of marijuana to heroin. Implicit in that minor amounts of marijuana are all right, but major amounts are not. Really what you are saying is that marijuana, trafficking or otherwise, is not worthy of our paying any attention to transporting it to the United States. Is that what you are saying? Am I not reading correctly between the lines?

**Mr. Miller.** I think we should differentiate between marijuana and heroin and between minor and major quantities of marijuana. One thing I was thinking when I said "minor" was this. Another man was arrested for half an ounce of marijuana on the beach. He received a sentence of five years and five months for half an ounce of marijuana. I definitely consider this a major sentence for a minor crime.

**Senator Biden.** I am not arguing on that. I am not even sure I do not agree with the implication I made. I was curious as to what you mean.

I do not know how anyone can say that 30 kilos is a minor amount of marijuana in terms of it being imported to the United

States. I can see how somebody would say that it makes no sense to make marijuana illegal and therefore it does not matter what you import.

If we are going to stick to the major-minor kind of qualifications, then I do not know how 30 kilos of anything is minor in terms of importation into the United States.

Anyway, that is neither here nor there.

Let me question you about the role of the American Consul. Did you attempt to contact the American Consul when you were arrested? Did you attempt to contact the American Embassy?

**Mr. Miller.** Yes. I asked numerous times to be allowed to speak with the American Consulate.

**Senator Biden.** Were you allowed to do that?

**Mr. Miller.** No. Not until much later.

**Senator Biden.** Did your mother attempt to contact the American Consul in Mexico in the area where you were being held?

**Mr. Miller.** My mother was not aware that I had been apprehended.

**Senator Biden.** She was when you asked for $5,000, wasn't she?

**Mr. Miller.** Yes. She did go to the American Consul. The transfer to the hospital was done with the help of the American Consul through pressure by my mother.

**Senator Biden.** In terms of getting a lawyer, that charlatan that stole the $5,000—had your mother, you, or anyone in your family contacted the American Consul prior to hiring that lawyer?

**Mr. Miller.** Yes. A man sent down by my family who spoke Spanish and English went to the American Consulate and asked about this attorney.

**Senator Biden.** What was the response?

**Mr. Miller.** Yes, that he was on the list as being one of the attorneys that was recommended.

**Senator Biden.** Do you recall who the American Consul was?

**Mr. Miller.** No, I do not know who the Consul was. I communicated with the Vice Consul.

**Senator Biden.** You spoke to the Vice Consul?

**Mr. Miller.** He came to the prison after I had been arrested. After 10 or 14 days he came to the prison to talk to me. He read me my rights.

**Senator Biden.** What did he tell you? Tell me about him.

**Mr. Miller.** He brought a list of attorneys and also something describing Mexican law. He read off where it said that under Mexican law, I had to be charged within 72 hours. I told him that I had been there over a week and that I was not charged for anything. I was incommunicado. He said he could not do anything about that.

It is also stated that you had to be tried and sentenced within one year. Going into the prison, I talked to a couple of Americans who had been in in prison over one year who had not been found guilty or not guilty.

There were a few other things pertaining to Mexican law and the list of attorneys which he told me about.

He asked me if I would like to contact my family and I told him my family had already been contacted.

**Senator Biden.** Do you feel that he was of any service with a positive consequence for you?

**Mr. Miller.** No, not really.

**Senator Biden.** Do you believe that this committee or any other committee should be looking into the role of the American Consul in those areas?

**Mr. Miller.** Yes, I definitely do. That is probably the case in any country. Americans would be helped.

**Senator Biden.** What do you think we should be asking them? If you were sitting here and if I had the American Consul before me or if you had him before you, what would you ask him?

**Mr. Miller.** I would ask him what their practice is with regard to Americans in need in foreign countries.

**Senator Biden.** He was on the other side of it.

**Mr. Miller.** In my particular experience, yes.

**Senator Biden.** What would you suggest? What is the line of questioning that you would address to the American Consul to make a record that they were good, bad, or indifferent?

**Mr. Miller.** I think—

**Senator Biden.** Is there anything they could have done for you that they did not do? Do you honestly believe it was in their power to do it and that it was denied you?

**Mr. Miller.** I cannot say for sure. I do not know whether they had any power or not. I think that they should have spoken to the authorities about the tortures, etc. I believe they should have talked to them about that.

There were other problems which we were facing, such as mail being stolen and checks sent by parents that were stolen.

We drew up a petition once and had it delivered to the American Consul. The mail had not arrived for over three weeks. We counted on this for survival to buy food and medical supplies. We found out that many of the checks had been cashed. We asked the American Consul to do something about it. It took a month. They said they were working and doing everything possible.

**Senator Biden.** Did you believe that?

**Mr. Miller.** I think the American Consul could do more if they really wanted to do more. I do not really think it was that big of a thing for them. I think it should be.

**Senator Biden.** Can you think of any instance where the American Consul did make a difference with you and/or with those with whom you served time?

**Mr. Miller.** For myself, they made a difference probably in saving my leg. I feel that it would have been amputated if I had not been transferred to a decent hospital. They did recommend a doctor. They worked with my mother and with the judge to have me transferred to a decent hospital.

**Senator Biden.** Was the treatment of you any different than a Mexican prisoner for a similar offense or a Mexican prisoner awaiting trial or a Mexican prisoner being held incommunicado? I am talking about your experience sitting in a jail. Were the Mexicans' treated any differently?

**Mr. Miller.** I believe everyone is treated differently. Probably being held incommunicado for seven days was not that common.

**Senator Biden.** You say it was not that common?

**Mr. Miller.** Yes, for Mexicans, it isn't that common. Their families know. In various ways within the prison itself, Americans are treated differently.

**Senator Biden.** Can you give me some examples of that?

**Mr. Miller.** We were constantly extorted. To give you an example of the extortion, the president of the commission would draw up a list of American prisoners who had paid money to buy space for shelter. He would come by and approach each American. By the way, there were no Mexicans on the list. He would tell us that we would be transferred to another section of the prison and we would lose everything that we paid for, including the friends we had made, and our routine would be upset unless we paid 500 pesos apiece to the commissioner. If we would pay 500 pesos, we would be able to stay.

Another time a list was drawn up of Americans. They called us in one at a time and said that they wanted a donation to help the warden's sick mother. They wanted 500 pesos apiece. Americans were the only ones on the list.

**Senator Biden.** Were your living conditions, the ones that you paid for, better than the average Americans or were they the same? Did all the Mexicans have carracas?

**Mr. Miller.** No. It did not matter whether you were a Mexican or an American. It mattered whether you had enough money to buy the hut. Some Mexicans had them and some Americans had them.

**Senator Biden.** Proportionately, were there more Americans, relative to their population in the prison, who had huts? Of all the carracas of which you were aware, what percentage were held by Mexicans and what percentage were held by Americans? Could you guess?

If there were 50 huts, then how many would have been held by Americans and how many would have been held by Mexicans?

**Mr. Miller.** I would say if there were 50 huts, then 15 Americans would have them. The population of Mexicans, of course, was greater.

**Senator Biden.** What was the factor, twice as many, even or what? Were you a distinct minority?

**Mr. Miller.** A distinct minority, yes. Out of 200 prisoners, there were 20 Americans, I would say.

**Senator Biden.** So the vast majority of Americans were able to purchase the huts but the vast majority of Mexicans were not able to purchase them. Is that right?

You were extorted, of course. Again, I am not trying to paint a picture of you having luxury while Mexicans wallowed in filth. It seems as though you all wallowed in filth. It seems as though the line of demarcation was how much money they had. Correct me if I am wrong.

**Mr. Miller.** That is it, exactly.

**Senator Biden.** Is there anything else you would like to add?

**Mr. Miller.** Nothing I can think of at this time.

**Senator Biden.** I have one last question.

If you were, in fact, in a Mexican prison—again, God forbid—and if you had committed a crime and if it was one that would be considered a major felony here in America, then do you think you would consider the consequences of returning home in terms of the impact that would have on your future and your ability to work and maintain friends and your daily routine? Would you weigh that at all against staying in a Mexican prison?

You would know that they might end up with a felony record here in the United States. They would be fingerprinted and photographed and so on. What kind of advice would you give someone like that? Would you consider those factors?

**Mr. Miller.** I do not know if I would actually advise anyone. I would tell them what they would be facing if they came home, and they probably would know what they are facing in Mexico. It would be an individual decision. It would depend on how much time a person had left on the record. You would have to consider the problems of employment in the United States.

**Senator Biden.** Let me ask you a callous question. If you were a very wealthy young man and your parents were very wealthy and if you had committed a crime which you felt pretty sure you would not be paroled for in the United States if you came back to the United States, and let's say you were sentenced to a time certain in Mexico, then would you be likely to be able to pay your way in the jail to make subsistence in that jail livable for you or to make it tolerable while you were facing a sentence rather than coming back to the United States? Are there any kings of the prison?

Are there people in the prison who are able to pay enough money so that they do not have to be subjected to the inhumanities that we have heard about today?

**Mr. Miller.** Yes, there were kings. There was one, in fact, but he was a Mexican. He was very wealthy, a big-time smuggler, I guess. He had his own room near the hospital ward. He went out drinking occasionally with the warden. Under those conditions, someone might want to remain.

**Senator Biden.** I want to thank you very much for your testimony. It has been most helpful.

# About the Author

Don Crowell Jr. is a UCLA graduate who loves to read and to write. He has traveled the world and has many of his own stories to tell. Being active in the film industry, Don has worked as story consultant, screenwriter, and movie producer. He lives with his wife, two daughters, three grandchildren, and the family dog, Budders.

*Don@noblehousebooks.com*